World Economic and Financial Surveys

Regional Economic Outlook

Western Hemisphere

· ·

NOV 07

INTERNATIONAL MONETARY FUND

Cataloging-in-Publication Data

Regional economic outlook : Western Hemisphere – [Washington, D.C.] : International

Monetary Fund, 2007.

p.   cm.   – (World economic and financial surveys)

Nov. 07.

Includes bibliographical references.

ISBN 978-1-58906-672-4

1. Economic forecasting – North America. 2. Economic forecasting – Latin America. 3. Economic forecasting – Caribbean Area. 4. North America – Economic conditions. 5. Latin America – Economic conditions – 1982- 6. Caribbean Area – Economic conditions – 1945- 7. North America – Economic conditions – Statistics. 8. Latin America – Economic conditions – 1982- – Statistics. 9. Caribbean Area – Economic conditions – 1945- – Statistics. I. International Monetary Fund. II. Series (World economic and financial surveys)

HC94 .R445 2007

Price: US$31.00
(US$26.00 to full-time faculty members
and students at universities and colleges)

Please send orders to:
International Monetary Fund, Publication Services
700 19th St. N.W., Washington, D.C. 20431, U.S.A.
Tel.: (202) 623-7430   Telefax: (202) 623-7201
E-mail: publications@imf.org
Internet: www.imf.org

Contents

Preface

This *Regional Economic Outlook: Western Hemisphere* was written by Roberto Benelli, Paul Cashin, Jingqing Chai, Marcello Estevão, Christopher Faircloth, Priyadarshani Joshi, Sanjaya Panth, Robert Rennhack, Ivanna Vladkova-Hollar, and Jeromin Zettelmeyer under the direction of Caroline Atkinson and Anoop Singh of the IMF's Western Hemisphere Department. Tamim Bayoumi, Fernando M. Gonçalves, Maria Lucia Guerra, Andreas Jobst, Herman Kamil, Pär Österholm, and Shaun Roache also contributed to specific aspects of the document, and economists in the IMF's Western Hemisphere, Monetary and Capital Markets, Fiscal, and Research Departments provided comments and data. Tom Duffy, Priyadarshani Joshi, Genevieve Lindow, Lita Ali, Joy Villacorte, and Carolina Worthington provided research and production assistance.

Executive Summary

Overview. The global context for countries in the Western Hemisphere is now influenced by the current weakness in the U.S. economy, stemming from the housing market, and its spillover effects in financial markets. Other external shocks are also affecting the Latin American and Caribbean (LAC) region, especially upward spikes in food prices, which have affected a number of countries this year. Against this background, this *Regional Economic Outlook: Western Hemisphere* is focused on the underlying resilience of the LAC region to shocks and the policy challenges involved in sustaining the region's improved fundamentals and, thereby, the current expansion.

Recent global and regional strength. The recent shocks have emerged after an exceptional period of strength both globally and for countries in the LAC region, which is helping contain the impact of the shifts in the external environment. Although the growth of the U.S. economy is now expected to slow to just under 2 percent for 2007–08, emerging market countries should retain sufficient momentum to keep global growth at a solid 4¾ percent in 2008 (Chapter 1). Indeed, the LAC region has, thus far, dealt well with the recent market turbulence, and domestic demand remains generally vigorous. Thus, the baseline scenario anticipates that growth across the LAC region should remain historically strong at close to 5 percent on average in 2007—the fourth year of uninterrupted, strong expansion—and continue at a robust 4¼ percent in 2008.

Latin America's social improvements. Latin America has made significant inroads during the current expansionary phase in bringing unemployment down to the single-digit range in most large countries and tackling the region's deep-seated poverty and inequality. Significantly, poverty in the region has declined much more rapidly during this expansion than in the 1990s, while inequality, although still high, has also declined in most countries since 1999 (Chapter 2).

Rising risks. Risks to the outlook, both domestic and external, lean clearly to the downside.

- As presented in the IMF's recent report on the *World Economic Outlook* (WEO), external risks, and uncertainty surrounding growth prospects, have recently increased. Among the risks are those related to growth in trading partners—especially the United States—and the persistence of abnormal conditions in credit markets.

- Within the LAC region, there are risks to the sustainability of the current expansion related to domestic as well as external factors, stemming from recent trends in government spending and credit growth, and their sustainability. In particular, fiscal and external surpluses are forecast to weaken, and inflation has been edging up—exacerbated by rising international food prices—as output has come closer to potential. Rising inflation in the region constitutes an important test, in some cases the first test, of the inflation targeting frameworks that have been adopted by a growing number of countries in the region.

Resilience. Drawing on new analytical work, this *Regional Economic Outlook* examines the region's resilience and looks to the domestic policy implications for sustaining the current expansion.

- *Resilience to external shocks* (Chapter 3). Compared with the 1990s, improved public and private sector balance sheets, lower and better anchored inflation expectations, and strengthened policy frameworks have made the region more resilient to changes in international financial conditions. Central banks, for example, can now respond to tighter international conditions with greater exchange rate flexibility than in the past. There has also been little indication as yet that banks in Latin America will retrench lending as a result of the recent market problems. However, Latin America remains acutely sensitive to pronounced weakness in external demand and to a possible deterioration in its terms of trade. New analytical work indicates that, in the event of a credit crunch and recession in the United States—combined with some spillover to world growth and a corresponding softening of commodity prices—2008 growth in the region could be reduced by up to 2 percentage points below the current baseline.

- *Strength of underlying fiscal positions* (Chapter 4). Fiscal primary surpluses in the LAC region rose further last year, driven by buoyant revenues. The question is whether these gains are permanent ("structural") or driven by cyclical conditions. A detailed analysis suggests that, for the most part, structural primary balances in the region remain in surplus. However, they are not as strong as headline primary balances would suggest, and are subject to large margins of uncertainty, in part because they depend on uncertain commodity price forecasts. Furthermore, revenue ratios are now projected to remain flat or decline modestly. If expenditures continue to grow at their current pace of 8–10 percent on average in real terms, primary fiscal surpluses—both headline and structural—will quickly turn to deficits in the coming years. In light of still-substantial debt levels in the region, the erosion of the fiscal position based on current expenditure trends is a significant concern.

- *Sustainability of credit growth* (Chapter 5). Recent average credit growth rates of almost 40 percent a year in the largest Latin American countries have raised questions about the sustainability of the ongoing boom in Latin America's financial sector. An analysis based on two alternative criteria for "excess" credit growth suggests, however, that much of the recent credit growth seems to be associated with improvements in fundamentals, rather than with significant overheating in the region as a whole. This finding is consistent with the latest prudential indicators and equity market–based bank solvency estimates, which show that nonperforming loan ratios and banks' estimated default probabilities have remained at low levels. However, the generally solid aggregate picture may mask heightened vulnerabilities in financial

REGIONAL ECONOMIC OUTLOOK: WESTERN HEMISPHERE

institutions that may have lowered credit standards in their pursuit of rapid expansion.

Policy challenges. Together, these risks raise significant short-term policy challenges, in addition to those related to long-term growth and equity. First and foremost, many Latin American countries would do well to significantly reduce the growth of current government spending, both to allow debt reduction to continue and to create room for more spending on capital improvements. This would also help Latin America's external current accounts, which are set to experience declining surpluses in coming years, as commodity prices have stabilized while imports continue to grow rapidly. Second, as widely recognized, the fast pace of credit growth in several countries requires enhanced regulatory oversight and strengthening of supervisory capacity. Third, with inflation edging up in many countries, monetary policy faces the challenge of striking a careful balance between continuing inflation concerns and the prospect of slowing external demand. Finally, the region faces the long-run challenge of raising investment and productivity toward levels of other fast-growing emerging market countries in order to sustain the recent upward trend in its potential GDP growth.

I. The Global Economy and the Outlook for the United States and Canada

Global Outlook

The global economy continues to grow strongly, although the recent turbulence in financial markets has reduced growth prospects for 2008 and increased downside risks. With vigorous growth in the first half of 2007, world output is now expected to expand by 5.2 percent this year before slowing to 4.8 percent in 2008 (see the October 2007 *World Economic Outlook*—WEO). As new information about sources of financial weaknesses in industrial economies has emerged, uncertainty about the future path of global economic activity has increased.

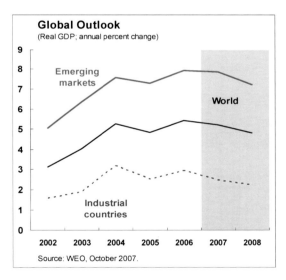

Global Outlook
(Real GDP; annual percent change)

Source: WEO, October 2007.

The global economy is being supported by a robust expansion in emerging market countries. In particular, emerging Asia is experiencing rapid growth in investment and output, led by China and India, which are expected to grow by 10 percent and 8½ percent, respectively, in 2008. This expansion in emerging market countries is counterbalancing more moderate growth in advanced countries. In the United States, growth is now projected at just below 2 percent in 2008, reflecting the continuing housing correction and the impact of the recent financial turmoil on confidence. The rate of expansion is expected to slow to 2.1 percent in the euro area and

1.7 percent in Japan on weaker external demand and tighter credit conditions. In response to these developments, monetary policy has been eased in the United States and the earlier tightening cycle has been put on hold in the euro area and Japan.

Inflation has edged down in industrial countries, but robust growth and higher commodity prices have led to price pressures in emerging market economies. For the advanced countries as a whole, inflation is expected to fall to 2 percent in 2008, while for developing and emerging markets consumer prices are projected to rise by 5.3 percent in 2008, after increasing by almost 6 percent in 2007. Petroleum price projections underlying the October 2007 WEO have been revised to an annual average of $68 in 2007 and $75 in 2008 and, with supply constraints biting, prices remain volatile. In line with futures markets, prices for metals and agricultural goods are also expected to remain elevated over the next few years, with high food prices reflecting booming biofuel production as well as rising demand from expanding emerging market economies.

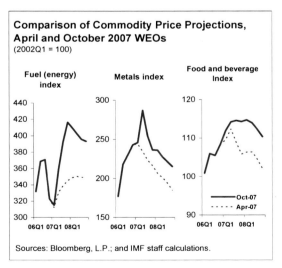

Comparison of Commodity Price Projections, April and October 2007 WEOs
(2002Q1 = 100)

Sources: Bloomberg, L.P.; and IMF staff calculations.

Growing concerns about exposure to the U.S. subprime market triggered global financial market turbulence in August that has unwound only partially (Box 1). While stock prices have generally recovered after initial sharp falls, spreads on short-term money market rates and debt instruments have remained elevated despite liquidity injections by major central banks. Industrial country high-yield bonds and asset-backed commercial paper have been hit harder than emerging market debt.

Against this background, the U.S. dollar has continued to depreciate against the euro, the Canadian dollar, and a broad range of other currencies, including those of emerging market countries. While the mix has varied by country, exchange market pressures in emerging markets have generally been reflected in exchange rate appreciation, rapid accumulation of international reserves, and strong domestic credit growth.

Outlook for the United States and Canada

Growth in the United States is projected to slow to 1.9 percent in 2007 and 2008, significantly below potential. This weakness largely reflects a continuation of the current downturn in the housing market. With housing starts and house price inflation continuing to drop rapidly, rising inventories and foreclosures suggest that residential investment will continue to subtract from growth during 2008. Consumption growth also slows as personal wealth is adversely affected by falling nominal house prices, exacerbated by the short-term impact of recent financial market strains on lending and confidence. External demand, however, should provide some cushion to activity as the combination of slower domestic activity and robust foreign growth boosts net exports.

The Federal Reserve (Fed) cut rates in mid-September to "help forestall some of the adverse effects on the broader economy that might otherwise arise from the disruptions in financial markets." The federal funds rate had earlier

Equity Markets in the U.S., Europe, and Japan
(January 3, 2005 = 100)

Source: Bloomberg, L.P.

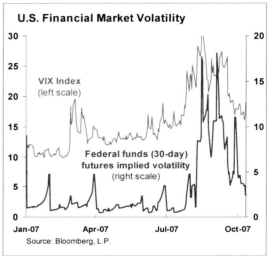

U.S. Financial Market Volatility

Source: Bloomberg, L.P.

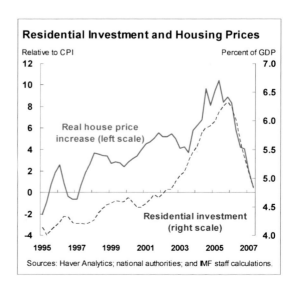

Residential Investment and Housing Prices

Sources: Haver Analytics; national authorities; and IMF staff calculations.

Box 1. Recent Financial Market Turmoil: What Happened, and Why?

Recent financial market liquidity problems can be traced to the search for yield during the low interest rate environment of 2005–06 and a loosening of credit standards, particularly in the U.S. subprime mortgage market. As investors worldwide sought higher yields, U.S. subprime originators faced strong incentives to expand the supply of loans. With many eager to participate in the housing boom but qualified individuals becoming scarcer, there was a rapid loosening of underwriting standards—including inadequate checking of credit quality, higher loan-to-value ratios, and "teaser" initial interest rates on adjustable rate mortgages—whose consequences rating agencies and regulators underestimated. As the U.S. housing market slowed, delinquencies on 2005 and 2006 subprime loans rose rapidly, and the value of the associated asset-backed instruments that were particularly sensitive to market conditions fell precipitously in early 2007.

While some risks were recognized, most observers expected the subprime crisis to be contained, as securitization had dispersed losses across the financial system. As described in Kiff and Mills (2007), the brunt of the crisis was initially borne by subprime lenders themselves, who were often contractually bound to take back loans from securitizers in cases of early payment defaults, and who, in any case, faced radically diminished business prospects as it became clear that the housing market was cooling. Many of these lenders went out of business in early 2007, with little effect on the banking system. There were some signs of concern, based around some hedge funds and other investors with substantial holdings of subprime mortgage-backed securities and the riskier tranches of subprime-based collateralized debt obligations (CDOs), including subsidiaries of Bear Sterns, a large U.S. investment bank.

In August, however, it became clear that the U.S. and European banking systems had significant, although not easily quantified, exposures to subprime losses through the asset-backed commercial paper market, leading to a more general loss of confidence. The delay in discovering the location of the subprime-related losses reflected the complexity of some of the structures into which pools of subprime loans had been placed (particularly CDOs); the illiquidity of the underlying markets, which made it difficult to obtain a market price; and the reluctance of the rating agencies to downgrade these instruments. When the rating agencies eventually downgraded a large number of asset-backed securities, however, it became clear that many of them had been bought by off-balance-sheet bank subsidiaries ("conduits") using short-term funds from the asset-backed commercial paper market.

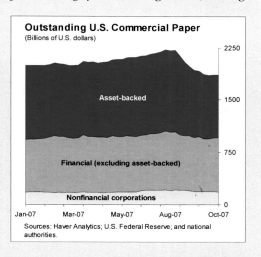

Outstanding U.S. Commercial Paper
(Billions of U.S. dollars)

Asset-backed

Financial (excluding asset-backed)

Nonfinancial corporations

Sources: Haver Analytics; U.S. Federal Reserve; and national authorities.

Lenders, realizing that the underlying assets were not sound, pulled out of asset-backed commercial paper market, triggering wide-ranging liquidity problems. As the commercial paper market shrank, U.S. and European banks were forced to provide lines of credit to these conduits and accept in return the impaired collateral.

_____

Note: This box was prepared by Tamim Bayoumi.

Box 1 *(concluded)*

The resulting uncertainty about the quality of banks' balance sheets led to a rapid increase in risk aversion, and investors' "flight to quality" led to a fall in yields on (particularly short-term) government paper, while spreads on investment-grade and (in particular) high-yield corporate debt rose sharply and equity markets plummeted across the globe. The interbank markets on both sides of the Atlantic experienced serious disruptions, with 1–6-month money essentially unavailable and shorter-term funds only available at a sizeable premium. In addition, in Canada, some banks were able to avoid supporting conduits, resulting in a standstill in parts of the commercial paper market.

U.S. Short-Term Interest Rates
(In percent)

— Three-month LIBOR
- - - Target federal funds rate
— Effective federal funds rate

Sources: Haver Analytics; and the U.S. Federal Reserve.

Central banks responded by providing liquidity at penalty rates. The U.S. Federal Reserve and, in particular, the European Central Bank used open market operations to inject substantial amounts of liquidity directly into markets. To further support market liquidity, the Fed also lowered its discount rate—at which it stands ready to lend directly to banks at a penalty spread while accepting a relatively wide range of collateral—eased terms of access, and allowed banks to increase temporarily loans to nonbank subsidiaries, above usually allowed limits.

However, liquidity in interbank markets remained tight. Despite ample provision of short-term funds, interbank lending at the 1–6-month term remained clogged. With concerns about counterparty risk lessening, banks appear to have been hoarding their cash in response to: high demand for loans, as borrowers activated contingent credit lines; uncertainty about cash needs, as commercial banks faced the prospect of honoring more off-balance-sheet commitments and investment banks of accommodating commitments for leveraged-buy-out-related loans; and, more speculatively, because banks wanted cash to buy distressed assets that will come into the market.

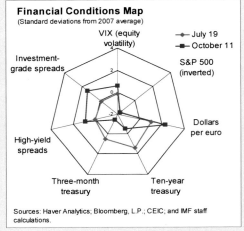

Financial Conditions Map
(Standard deviations from 2007 average)

◆ July 19
■ October 11

VIX (equity volatility)
S&P 500 (inverted)
Dollars per euro
Ten-year treasury
Three-month treasury
High-yield spreads
Investment-grade spreads

Sources: Haver Analytics; Bloomberg, L.P.; CEIC; and IMF staff calculations.

In response, on September 18, the Fed lowered the federal funds rate by 50 basis points to help offset the negative impact on the macroeconomy. With U.S. banks' demand for cash remaining high, however, money market conditions remain difficult and it may take some time for interbank markets to return to full liquidity, while in Canada the standstill in the asset-backed commercial paper market has yet to be resolved. More generally, there appears to have been a global repricing of risk, implying that spreads on risky instruments are unlikely to return to levels seen in recent years, with negative consequences for global activity. On October 15, three major financial institutions, Citigroup, Bank of America, and JPMorgan Chase, agreed to set up a fund of as much as $80 billion to help revive the asset-backed commercial paper market, although it is still too early to see the effect of this step.

been kept at a mildly restrictive 5¼ percent since mid-2006 despite slowing growth, allowing core inflation to decelerate from an uncomfortably high 2.5 percent early this year to 1.8 percent in September. The Fed initially reacted to financial market turmoil in August with substantial liquidity injections, waiting until the next scheduled meeting of the federal open markets committee on September 19 to cut the federal funds rate by 50 basis points. While financial conditions have improved recently, with equity markets hitting new highs in October, money market strains have continued, most notably in 1–6-month interbank markets. On October 31, 2007, the federal funds rate target was reduced by a further 25 basis points, to 4½ percent.

In the baseline scenario, the drag on growth from the housing sector gradually lessens through 2008 while consumption is supported by solid labor market fundamentals. Overall, annualized GDP growth is projected to recover from 1½ percent in the fourth quarter of 2007 to just above 2½ percent a year later. Pressures on core inflation are expected to ease further, driven by a widening output gap and a slowing in the cost of shelter.

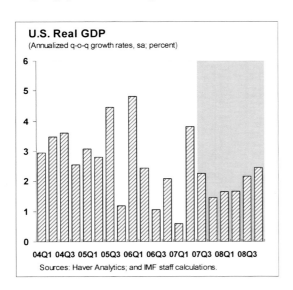

U.S. Real GDP
(Annualized q-o-q growth rates, sa; percent)

Sources: Haver Analytics; and IMF staff calculations.

Risks to this already modest U.S. growth outlook are clearly tilted to the downside for three main reasons. First, the housing downturn could be even deeper than currently projected, leading to weaker residential investment and larger knock-on effects on wealth and consumption. Second, the ongoing financial market strains could lead to a substantial and extended tightening in financing conditions, further dampening consumption and investment growth. Third, there is the risk that the recent slowing of productivity growth could be more permanent and structural in nature than expected, which, through expectations of lower future income, would also reduce consumption and investment spending.

At unchanged real exchange rates, the current account deficit is projected to decline further to 5¾ percent of GDP in 2007 and 5½ percent in 2008, despite continued high oil prices. This largely reflects the impact of the slowdown on the demand for imports, and the external deficit could improve further if downside risks to activity to materialize. Turning to financing, if foreign investors maintain their recent caution about purchasing U.S. assets then it is possible that the recent weakening in the value of the dollar will continue as funding costs rise.

Continuing the trend seen in recent years, fiscal developments have remained favorable, with the federal government deficit in FY 2007 improving by ¾ percentage point of GDP to 1¼ percent of GDP. The overperformance primarily reflects strong revenue buoyancy but also slower-than-expected spending execution. The deficit is expected to increase modestly in FY 2008 (which started in October) as revenue buoyancy tapers off and spending rebounds. The key fiscal challenge remains reforming unsustainable entitlement programs, preferably combined with a more stringent medium-term fiscal target, such as budget balance excluding the social security surplus.

In Canada, growth has remained buoyant, although some slowing is projected for 2008. Strong domestic demand and substantial terms of trade gains—on account of increasing commodity prices—have supported the economy, and the unemployment rate has declined to a 33-year low of 6.0 percent. Slower U.S. growth and financial market difficulties are likely to dampen activity

moving forward, and annual growth is projected
to slow to 2.5 percent in 2007 and 2.3 percent in
2008. Risks to the near-term growth outlook for
Canada are also on the downside, largely reflecting
possibly weaker U.S. prospects but also concerns
about domestic financial conditions and currency
appreciation.

The global liquidity squeeze has adversely affected
Canada's interbank market, notwithstanding
conservative regulatory and business practices that
minimized the initial impact of financial volatility
on the balance sheets of major banks. About one-
third of the asset-backed commercial paper
market—equivalent to 2½ percent of GDP—was
put into a standstill in August. If this standstill is
not resolved quickly, there are concerns that
money market liquidity conditions could tighten
further. Against this backdrop, interest rates were
left on hold in early September even though the
economy was still operating above potential.
Nevertheless, with domestic demand set to
weaken, inflation is expected to moderate back to
the midpoint of the Bank of Canada's 1–3 percent
target range, after a pickup in late 2006 and early
2007.

The commodity-related terms of trade gains have
also strengthened the external current account
surplus, which is projected at 1.8 percent of GDP
in 2007 and 1.2 percent in 2008. At the same time,
the Canadian dollar, which is widely considered to
be a commodity currency, has risen to parity

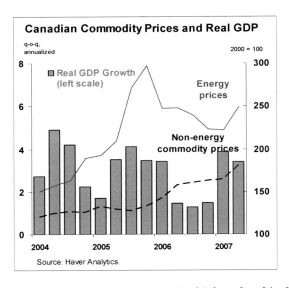

Canadian Commodity Prices and Real GDP

Source: Haver Analytics.

against its U.S. counterpart—its highest level in 30
years. In real effective terms, the Canadian dollar
has now appreciated by some 45 percent from its
low in early 2002. This real appreciation largely
reflects higher commodity prices. But recent
strength—with appreciation of 5 percentage
points in the last three months alone— may well
reflect momentum effects in an environment of
generalized U.S. dollar weakness. While the
appreciation has adversely affected manufacturing,
the Canadian economy has adjusted smoothly to
currency strength overall, with flexible labor
markets supporting employment gains in services,
construction, and mining that more than offset
losses in manufacturing.

II. The Outlook for Latin America and the Caribbean

Overall Developments and Prospects

The region has weathered the recent market turbulence well so far and the economic outlook for 2007–08 remains generally robust. However, downward risks to the growth outlook have increased, and there are some signs that the improved fundamentals underpinning the region's resilience may erode if policies do not strengthen. While inflation has remained generally low, it has recently been edging up in many countries. Fiscal and current account surpluses are shrinking as public spending and imports continue to rise strongly.

The sustainability of the expansion will depend crucially on external conditions, the strength of underlying fiscal positions, the resilience of domestic financial sectors, and containing inflation. New analytical work on these issues is summarized in this chapter and presented in more detail in the three thematic chapters that follow.

The LAC region continued to expand vigorously in the first half of this year after a strong performance in 2006, the best in many years for a number of countries. The shift in global conditions since midyear will likely slow growth somewhat next year from the 5 percent average projected for 2007. However, under the baseline for world growth in the IMF's WEO, the expansion is forecast to remain relatively robust, at 4¼ percent on average in 2008—the fifth year of continuous growth in excess of 4 percent. Countries with closer links to the United States (such as Mexico and those in Central America) are expected to be more affected by the projected slowdown in the United States.

Economic activity has strengthened in several countries in which growth was relatively subdued last year, particularly in Brazil, where year-on-year growth reached a high of 5½ percent in the second quarter. In most other countries, the expansion remained vigorous and in some cases continued to set historical records. Even after the midyear financial market turbulence, commodity prices have stayed strong, supporting economic

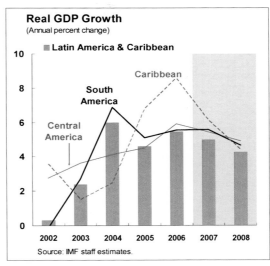

Real GDP Growth
(Annual percent change)

Source: IMF staff estimates.

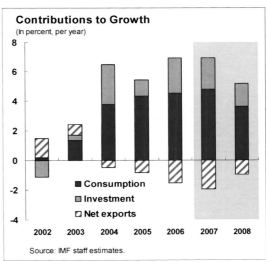

Contributions to Growth
(In percent, per year)

Source: IMF staff estimates.

activity in commodity-exporting countries such as Peru and Bolivia. In Colombia and Uruguay, growth has been driven mainly by domestic demand but has also benefited from strong exports. A good 2007 harvest helped boost this year's output in Argentina and Paraguay. Looking ahead, growth is expected to moderate next year relative to 2007 in most countries, reflecting the external environment and in some cases supply constraints. Growth in 2008 is expected to be in the 3–4 percent range in Mexico, Ecuador, and Uruguay; the 4–5 percent range in Brazil, Chile,

Colombia, and Paraguay; and in the 5½-6 percent range in Argentina, Bolivia, Peru, and Venezuela.

Growth in Central America also remained strong in the first half of 2007. Although the slowdown in the United States, the region's main trading partner, is expected to have a significant dampening effect, output is still projected at just under 5 percent on average in 2008. Macroeconomic and political stability and the implementation of Central American Free Trade Agreement-Dominican Republic (CAFTA-DR)—which has now been ratified by all Central American countries, following the referendum in Costa Rica in October—are boosting investment and the growth of nontraditional exports in the region. Further rises in remittances (albeit recently at slower rates, see Chapter 3) have bolstered consumption. The economic expansion has been particularly vigorous in Costa Rica and Panama.

Output Growth
(In percent; annual rate)

	1995-2004 Avg.	2005	2006	2007 Proj.	2008 Proj.
Central America 1/	**3.7**	**4.5**	**5.9**	**5.4**	**4.9**
Costa Rica	4.3	5.9	8.2	6.0	5.0
El Salvador	3.0	3.1	4.2	4.2	3.8
Guatemala	3.4	3.5	4.9	4.8	4.3
Honduras	3.3	4.1	6.0	5.4	3.4
Nicaragua	4.3	4.4	3.7	4.2	4.7
Panama	4.4	6.9	8.1	8.5	8.8

Source: WEO.
1/ PPP-weighted average.

In most of the Caribbean, growth has also been robust and is expected to remain strong by historical standards, despite some slowdown since 2006. Trinidad and Tobago is expected to continue to expand at more sustainable rates during 2007–08 (around 6 percent), as capacity constraints are emerging following several years of rapid growth. Growth in the Dominican Republic, which has been boosted by strong consumption and tourism-related investment, is expected to slow to 8 percent in 2007 and 4½–5½ percent in 2008. In the Eastern Caribbean Currency Union (ECCU) area, growth is projected at around 3½ percent during 2007–08, while Guyana's

growth is currently running at 5 percent, compared with negligible growth during 2002–05.

Recent natural disasters have extracted a high toll in human suffering, but their economic effects are likely to be limited, except in some Caribbean countries. In Peru, preliminary estimates for the impact of an earthquake in August 2007 suggest damages in the range of ⅓–½ percent of GDP. In Nicaragua, a hurricane caused significant dislocations in the sparsely populated northeast, but the aggregate economic impact appears contained so far. However, Hurricane Dean hit several Eastern Caribbean countries hard, particularly Dominica, where it caused damage of at least 15 percent of GDP. In Jamaica, hurricane effects are slowing production and raising food price inflation.

While recent financial turbulence has only modestly reduced the region's baseline growth outlook, it has significantly increased downward risks. The main sources of macroeconomic risk for the region—discussed in greater detail in Chapter 3—stem from weaker external growth, the potential for a further tightening in U.S. and global credit markets, and the negative impact that weaker-than-expected global demand could have on commodity prices. In a few countries, including Argentina, Honduras, and Nicaragua, energy shortages could also create risks to the growth outlook. On the upside, domestic demand

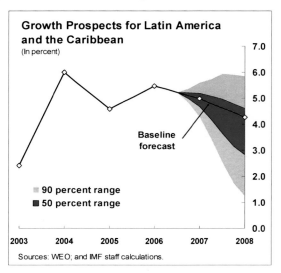

Growth Prospects for Latin America and the Caribbean
(In percent)

Baseline forecast

■ 90 percent range
■ 50 percent range

Sources: WEO; and IMF staff calculations.

could expand faster than currently expected. The fan chart for the region's growth prospects, based on the analysis in Chapter 3, summarizes the risks to the outlook. Significantly lower growth than currently projected remains a definite possibility. But a full-fledged recession in the region (with average annual growth falling to 1 percent or less) continues to be very unlikely.

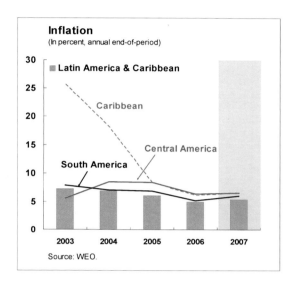

Inflation
(In percent, annual end-of-period)

Source: WEO.

Inflation remains contained by historical standards. Nonetheless, following an historical low in 2006 for the region as a whole, inflation rates have recently been edging up in many countries. This reflects both the cyclical expansion in the region and, in several countries, the impact of a global rise in food prices (see the October 2007 *World Economic Outlook*, Chapter 1). In some countries, little upward flexibility in nominal exchange rates has limited disinflation effects that might have operated through this channel.

In Colombia and Uruguay, inflation has risen in the context of vigorous growth, and is approaching or exceeding the upper end of central bank targets. In Chile, Mexico, and Peru, headline inflation remains contained but food price inflation has forced it above central banks' targets. Inflation also has been ticking up in some countries of Central America and the Caribbean, remains high in Argentina, has recently moved into the double digits in Bolivia (on a 12-month basis), and has stayed well in the double digits in

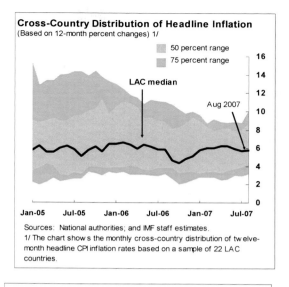

Cross-Country Distribution of Headline Inflation
(Based on 12-month percent changes) 1/

Sources: National authorities; and IMF staff estimates.
1/ The chart shows the monthly cross-country distribution of twelve-month headline CPI inflation rates based on a sample of 22 LAC countries.

Inflation
(In percent; end of period rate) 1/

	1995-2004 Avg.	2005	2006	2007 Proj.
North America 2/	**3.3**	**3.3**	**2.6**	**3.3**
United States	2.5	3.4	2.5	3.3
Canada	1.9	2.2	1.3	2.6
Mexico	15.5	3.3	4.1	3.6
South America 2/	**9.5**	**6.8**	**5.2**	**6.0**
Argentina	4.9	12.3	9.8	10.0
Bolivia	5.0	4.9	5.0	10.4
Brazil	7.3	5.7	3.1	4.0
Chile	4.2	3.7	2.6	5.5
Colombia	12.0	4.9	4.5	5.0
Ecuador	31.4	3.1	2.9	2.3
Paraguay	8.9	9.9	12.5	5.0
Peru	4.9	1.5	1.1	2.7
Uruguay	14.0	4.9	6.4	8.3
Venezuela	35.1	14.4	17.0	17.0
Central America 2/	**7.8**	**8.4**	**6.3**	**6.5**
Costa Rica	12.4	14.1	9.4	9.0
El Salvador	4.0	4.3	4.9	4.0
Guatemala	7.4	8.6	5.8	6.0
Honduras	13.4	7.7	5.3	8.0
Nicaragua	8.5	9.6	9.5	7.3
Panama	0.9	3.4	2.2	4.4
The Caribbean 2/	**11.0**	**8.3**	**6.1**	**6.5**
Latin America and the Caribbean 2/	**10.6**	**6.1**	**5.0**	**5.4**

Source: WEO.
1/ End-of-period rates, i.e. December on December. These will generally differ from period average inflation rates quoted in the *World Economic Outlook*, although both are based on identical underlying projections.
2/ PPP-weighted average.

Venezuela despite the relaxing of some supply constraints through imports. In Brazil, inflation remains below the midpoint of the target range but has also risen recently.

Rising food prices since mid-2006 have contributed to inflationary pressures in many countries, with the median differential between 12-month food and headline inflation rates reaching 3¾ percent by August 2007. This has affected large countries (especially Brazil, Chile, Colombia, and Mexico) but also the smaller ones in Central America and the Caribbean. In response, some governments have taken steps to curb food-price pressures directly. For example, competition has been encouraged by liberalizing food imports further in Guyana, Mexico, and Uruguay. Other steps have included reducing the VAT rate (Venezuela), introducing temporary VAT exemptions (Uruguay), and prohibiting exports of some food products (Argentina). In Mexico, the government also negotiated with the private sector to limit price increases of several staple items.

Inflation has also been driven by aggregate demand pressures and closing output gaps (Box 2). Rapid import growth also indicates that domestic demand is rising faster than production capacity in many countries. A further indication that short-run supply constraints are beginning to bind comes from unemployment rates. These have declined steadily in the past few years. However, the pace of decline has recently slowed, suggesting that unemployment may now largely reflect structural bottlenecks (see the November 2006 *Regional Economic Outlook: Western Hemisphere*—henceforth, *Regional Economic Outlook*—Box 9).

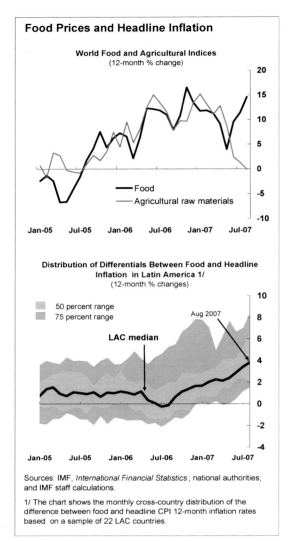

Sources: IMF, *International Financial Statistics*; national authorities; and IMF staff calculations.

1/ The chart shows the monthly cross-country distribution of the difference between food and headline CPI 12-month inflation rates based on a sample of 22 LAC countries.

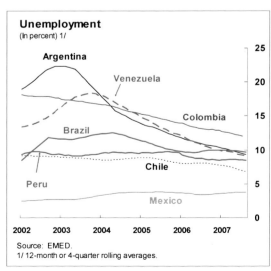

Source: EMED.
1/ 12-month or 4-quarter rolling averages.

Box 2. Latin America's Cyclical Position

Since 2004, Latin America has been growing at its fastest rate (over 5 percent a year on average) since the 1970s, helping to reduce unemployment significantly in many countries. Robust economic activity has been widespread across the region and economic fundamentals point to continued vigor in the coming years. While growth has been broad based, inflation performance has varied more markedly within the region. For instance, in Argentina and Venezuela inflation rates are in the double digits, while in Brazil they have been below the central bank targets, albeit rising recently. This suggests the existence of resource constraints in some countries, although not in all.

This box presents estimates of the cyclical position of Latin American countries—the commonly used output gap, which represents deviation of actual output from its cyclically neutral position—and sheds some light on the extent of resource constraints in the region. An estimate of the region's cyclical position informs the view on inflationary pressures, and also provides an input for fiscal structural balance calculations (see Chapter 4).

Measuring the output gap

The output gap is defined as the difference between actual (Y) and potential output (Y^*) as a proportion of potential output, $(Y–Y^*)/Y^*$. The concept of potential output should be understood as the production level at which the economy is in a cyclically neutral position. While not directly observable, the potential output of an economy can be estimated by different methodologies.

A commonly used method relies on applying a statistical filter on the output series to separate trend from cyclical variations. Econometricians have provided many different procedures to separate these two components, and here we use several of them. The filters used are the ones proposed by Hodrick and Prescott (1997), Baxter and King (1999), Christiano and Fitzgerald (2003), and the frequency domain approach of Corbae and Ouliaris (2002, 2006).

A well-known alternative method uses a production function framework to estimate potential output. In this framework, first, the contribution of observable inputs—capital and labor—to the production process is subtracted from output (using estimated weights for each factor) to produce a measure of total factor productivity. Then, a statistical filter, like the ones proposed by the authors listed above, is used to separate cyclical from trend variations in capital, labor, and total factor productivity. The potential output series is obtained by using a weighted average of the filtered production input series.[1]

Latin America's cyclical position

Using the first method, statistical filters are applied to annual data for all Latin American countries from

---

Note: This box was prepared by Marcello Estevão, Maria Lucia Guerra, and Jeromin Zettelmeyer.

[1] The calculation assumes constant returns of scale and can be written as $\ln(TFP) = \ln(Y) – \alpha * \ln(K) – (1–\alpha) * \ln(L)$, where TFP, Y, K, and L stand for total factor productivity, output, the capital stock, and employment. The parameter α varies somewhat across countries and, unless estimates were provided by a particular paper or by country authorities, was approximated by using the share of labor income in total value added, a method pioneered by Solow (1957).

The results from the two approaches will tend to be similar as, ultimately, statistical filters are used to parse out cyclical fluctuations either directly on the output series or on the input series. However, small variations may appear depending on the relative trend estimates for each production input. Also, the production function approach can be extended to include a more detailed breakdown of inputs into variables with strong policy content (e.g., capital utilization, unemployment rate, and labor force participation).

Box 2 *(concluded)*

1970 to 2010, using IMF staff forecasts as presented in the October 2007 *World Economic Outlook*, for the period 2007–10. The inclusion of these observations helps to attenuate the end-of-sample problem present in several of the statistical filters used here.

Two measures of the output gap in Latin America are then obtained: one by aggregating country-level information and another one by applying the filters directly to an aggregate output series for Latin America. As both series have similar cyclical properties, the chart shows only the latter measure. The output gap measure shows the expected troughs (during the 1982–84 and 1994 debt crises, for instance) and peaks. Using staff estimates for 2007, the data suggest that Latin America as a whole now faces a slightly positive output gap and a potential growth rate of about 4.7 percent.

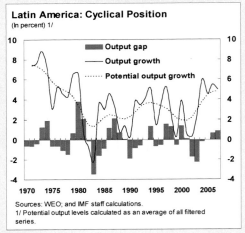

Latin America: Cyclical Position
(In percent) 1/

Sources: WEO; and IMF staff calculations.
1/ Potential output levels calculated as an average of all filtered series.

This aggregate information masks cross-country heterogeneity. Among the large Latin American economies, Argentina and Venezuela present wider positive output gaps, corroborating the perception from rising inflation pressures in those countries that they have been facing significant resource constraints. Output gaps are also positive in Colombia and, in some estimates, in Mexico and Peru. The Brazilian and Chilean economies are estimated to be in cyclically neutral positions in 2006/07.

The production function approach could only be applied to a selected group of countries with readily available data. Also, the resulting estimates suffer from the end-period problem common in some filtering techniques, as forecasts for production inputs are not available. Nonetheless, output gap estimates using this approach tend to present the same cyclical properties as the first set of estimates discussed above. Important differences

LAC Countries: Output Gap Estimates, 2006-07

(In percent of potential output)

Country	Year	Potential Output Estimation Method 1/			Production Function Approach 2/
		HP	BK	OC	
Jamaica	2006	0.3	-0.5	0.9	-0.9
	2007	-0.1	-0.2	0.8	...
Costa Rica	2006	1.2	0.8	1.4	1.2
	2007	1.2	0.9	1.0	...
Argentina	2006	2.5	1.2	2.7	...
	2007	2.8	1.8	2.3	...
Brazil	2006	-0.1	-0.4	0.0	-1.7
	2007	0.3	0.0	0.4	-1.1
Chile	2006	-0.2	-0.3	0.9	-1.1
	2007	0.4	-0.1	-0.1	-0.3
Colombia	2006	0.6	0.6	0.4	1.0
	2007	1.5	0.8	1.0	1.5
Mexico	2006	0.8	0.4	2.8	...
	2007	0.3	0.2	2.6	...
Peru	2006	0.8	0.9	-0.7	0.0
	2007	1.2	0.8	-1.0	0.5
Venezuela	2006	3.4	3.8	2.9	...
	2007	3.5	3.7	2.1	...

1/ Statistical filters applied directly on output figures. Sample: annual data 1970-2010. The table shows a subset of all estimated filters. Abbreviations used: HP = Hodrick-Prescott; BK = Baxter-King. HP sets lambda at 6.25.
2/ Filters applied to input series (capital, labor, and total factor productivity), which are then aggregated according to production function weights for each input.

between the two sets of results include a more positive output gap for Argentina and negative, but shrinking in absolute size, estimates for Brazil and Chile.[2]

---

[2] A third approach is currently being developed by IMF staff. It consists of backing out the size of the output gap using a small open-economy neo-Keynesian model consisting of equations for a Phillips curve, aggregate demand, uncovered interest parity, and an interest rate rule, as discussed in Berg, Karam, and Laxton (2006). The model is estimated using Bayesian techniques and an unobserved-components specification to identify the output gap, under the assumption that potential output is the production level consistent with stable inflation. An application for Mexico shows reduced inflation persistence in recent years, a moderate degree of pass-through from exchange rate depreciation to inflation, and a sluggish interest rate response to the cycle. Overall, the fit of the model reflects fairly well the recent disinflation episode in the country and suggests that the Mexican economy was at its potential in early 2007, a result consistent with most statistical filters used here.

Financial Sector Developments

The recent global financial turmoil came at a time of robust growth in the region's financial sector activities. Private sector credit in Latin America has been growing strongly for several years. Equity and local debt markets have generally seen increases in prices and trading volume, and derivatives markets and securitization have developed significantly in some countries.

During the global turbulence of July/August, market corrections were also observed across Latin America. These tended to be larger in countries with recent sharp market gains:

- Following a peak around late July, equity prices fell between 10 percent and 28 percent across the region. Declines were particularly marked in Brazil, Argentina, Colombia, Mexico, Chile, and Peru. However, prices have since recovered, surpassing their pre-turbulence levels in several countries.

- Similarly, while most currencies depreciated initially (between 1 percent and 14 percent in the larger economies), they have since tended to appreciate again.

- Local bond prices fell and sovereign spreads rose, but in most cases by much less than in the crises of the 1990s and the early years of this decade. In Brazil, Chile, Colombia, Mexico, and Peru, for example, sovereign spreads rose by less than 100 basis points between mid-July and the peak of the turbulence, and had returned to within 30 basis points of their mid-July levels by mid-October.

- Unlike in industrial economies, where the direct exposure to the U.S. mortgage market was higher and liquidity in money markets dried up, most countries in the region did not face liquidity problems in local markets.

Before the global turbulence, credit to the private sector was growing rapidly. This trend is expected

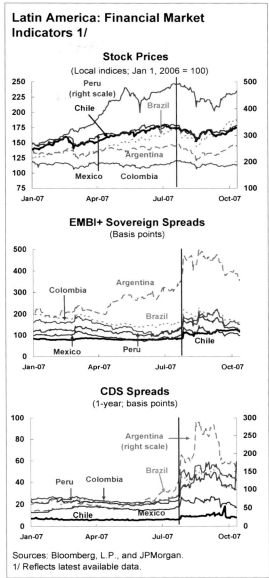

Latin America: Financial Market Indicators 1/

Sources: Bloomberg, L.P., and JPMorgan.
1/ Reflects latest available data.

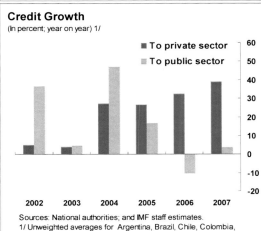

Credit Growth
(In percent; year on year) 1/

Sources: National authorities; and IMF staff estimates.
1/ Unweighted averages for Argentina, Brazil, Chile, Colombia, Mexico, Peru, and Venezuela. For 2007, rates are based on latest available data.

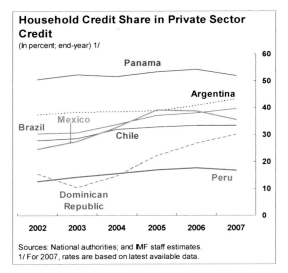

Household Credit Share in Private Sector Credit
(In percent; end-year) 1/

Sources: National authorities; and IMF staff estimates.
1/ For 2007, rates are based on latest available data.

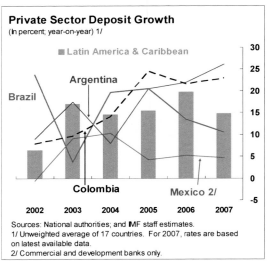

Private Sector Deposit Growth
(In percent; year-on-year) 1/

Sources: National authorities; and IMF staff estimates.
1/ Unweighted average of 17 countries. For 2007, rates are based on latest available data.
2/ Commercial and development banks only.

Cross-Border Claims of BIS Reporting Banks on Domestic Banking Sector

	In billions of U.S. dollars		As percent of total liabilities	
	2002	2006	2002	2006
Latin America	**30.1**	**52.1**	**6.2**	**4.8**
Argentina	2.6	1.9	5.1	2.6
Brazil	9.9	21.7	3.5	2.6
Chile	3.1	6.8	6.5	6.5
Colombia	1.2	1.8	5.6	3.8
Costa Rica	0.8	1.1	9.6	7.7
Mexico	5.5	9.4	2.5	1.6
Panama	1.7	3.1	8.1	10.4
Peru	2.0	1.0	8.7	3.3
Uruguay	0.4	0.6	3.7	4.5
Venezuela 1/	0.7	1.7	4.5	3.9

Sources: Bank of International Settlements; and IMF, *International Financial Statistics*.
1/ June data for 2006 for Venezuela.

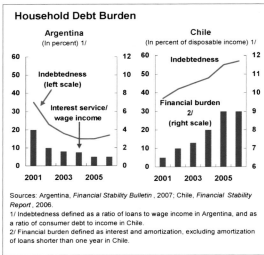

Household Debt Burden

Sources: Argentina, *Financial Stability Bulletin*, 2007; Chile, *Financial Stability Report*, 2006.
1/ Indebtedness defined as a ratio of loans to wage income in Argentina, and as a ratio of consumer debt to income in Chile.
2/ Financial burden defined as interest and amortization, excluding amortization of loans shorter than one year in Chile.

to continue, but with some slowing as monetary policy has tightened in many countries and global credit conditions have become less favorable. In the first half of 2007, credit was up by over 40 percent from a year earlier in the seven largest Latin American countries, and by over 20 percent in the region as a whole. The marked expansion in private sector credit since 2004 has been driven mostly by household credit, which currently accounts for about 40 percent of private sector credit outstanding. More recently, corporate credit growth has accelerated and may have surpassed household credit growth in several countries. In contrast, credit to the public sector has further contracted, reflecting improved fiscal positions. Credit expansion in the region has been funded largely by robust growth in local private deposits.

While foreign borrowing by local offices of international banks has also played a role in countries such as Panama, Costa Rica, and Chile, foreign liabilities generally account for a small and declining share of banking systems' total liabilities.

At this point, there do not seem to be clear signs of increased vulnerabilities as a result of the private sector credit expansion. While the capital adequacy ratio declined slightly in 2006–07, the nonperforming loan ratio has continued to fall, with increased provisioning and improved profitability. In Argentina and Chile, where data for household debt burden are available, indebtedness is within reasonable ranges. In Mexico, households have a net positive financial position of around 23 percent of GDP, contrasting with their near–net debtor position

Financial Soundness Indicators for Latin America
(In percent) 1/

	2002	2003	2004	2005	2006	2007 2/
NPL ratio 3/	10.5	8.7	5.2	3.8	2.9	3.1
Provisioning of NPLs	92.0	101.1	114.1	125.0	137.0	129.4
Return on assets	-0.4	1.2	1.6	1.8	1.9	2.0
Return on equity	3.7	10.2	15.4	18.6	21.2	21.5
Capital adequacy ratio	15.3	15.8	16.2	15.4	14.9	15.2
Liquid asset ratio	24.1	26.7	28.2	26.4	25.0	26.4

Source: IMF (2007a).
1/ Unweighted averages. Fixed sample of countries over time for each indicator. The number of countries varies by indicator.
2/ Latest data available.
3/ Nonperforming loans (NPLs) as a share of total loans.
4/ Regulatory capital/risk weighted assets.

New Listings in Latin America

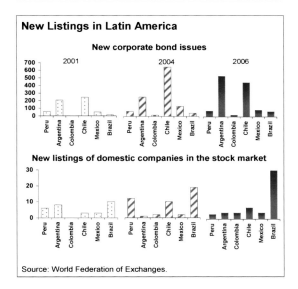

New corporate bond issues

New listings of domestic companies in the stock market

Source: World Federation of Exchanges.

during the 1995 crisis (Guerra de Luna and Serrano Bandala, 2007). Finally, a new empirical analysis for identifying excessive credit booms, based on commonly used criteria supports the view that, so far, recent credit growth seems to be associated mostly with improved fundamentals (Chapter 5). This said, prudential indicators are of course backward looking and household debt data are limited in most countries. Furthermore, the aggregate picture may mask heightened vulnerabilities in financial institutions that have lowered credit standards in their pursuit of rapid expansion. The rapid pace of credit growth in some countries hence warrants enhanced regulatory oversight.

In many countries in the region, financial intermediation remains below that in other emerging market countries. However, the main markets have recently experienced growing trading volume, as well as higher valuations, and rises in corporate stock and bond issues. Derivatives activities in foreign exchange and interest rates have continued to expand in the larger local markets, with total outstanding volume reaching US$16 billion in the first half of 2006 for LAC markets, up from US$4 billion in 1999 (JPMorgan, 2007).

External Developments

Despite generally favorable terms of trade and improving export performance, a strong rise in imports is driving down the regional current account surplus. Notwithstanding recent episodes of portfolio inflows to a few countries, foreign direct investment (FDI) generally remains the main source of foreign capital.

The region's external current account surplus is expected to contract significantly in 2007–08 after reaching a record high last year. High import volume growth, especially in Argentina, Brazil,

External Current Account
(In percent of GDP)

	1995-2004 Avg.	2005	2006	2007 Proj.	2008 Proj.
North America 1/	**-3.0**	**-5.1**	**-5.2**	**-4.8**	**-4.7**
United States	-3.3	-6.1	-6.2	-5.7	-5.5
Canada	0.8	2.0	1.6	1.8	1.2
Mexico	-2.1	-0.6	-0.3	-0.7	-1.1
South America 1/	**-2.1**	**1.3**	**1.5**	**0.7**	**0.3**
Argentina	-0.5	1.9	2.5	0.9	0.4
Bolivia	-3.8	6.5	11.7	15.1	9.9
Brazil	-2.4	1.6	1.2	0.8	0.3
Chile	-1.8	1.1	3.6	3.7	2.3
Colombia	-2.4	-1.5	-2.1	-3.9	-3.5
Ecuador	-1.8	0.8	3.6	2.4	2.5
Paraguay	-1.7	0.1	-2.0	-0.2	-0.3
Peru	-3.7	1.4	2.8	1.3	1.1
Uruguay	-1.1	0.0	-2.4	-2.8	-2.8
Venezuela	6.5	17.8	15.0	7.8	4.1
Central America 1/	**-5.1**	**-5.1**	**-5.0**	**-5.6**	**-5.8**
Costa Rica	-3.9	-4.8	-4.9	-4.8	-5.0
El Salvador	-2.4	-4.6	-4.7	-4.9	-5.0
Guatemala	-5.2	-5.1	-5.2	-5.1	-4.7
Honduras	-3.8	-0.9	-1.6	-5.5	-5.0
Nicaragua	-20.4	-14.9	-15.8	-15.8	-16.3
Panama	-5.3	-5.0	-3.8	-5.4	-6.6
The Caribbean 1/	**-3.4**	**-0.3**	**-0.4**	**-1.0**	**-0.6**
Latin America and the Caribbean 1/	**-2.0**	**1.4**	**1.5**	**0.6**	**0.0**

Source: WEO.
1/ Dollar-weighted GDP average.

External Balance of Payments Developments
(In percent of GDP, unless otherwise indicated) 1/

	2003	2004	2005	2006	2007 2/	2008 2/
Trade balance	1.7	2.2	2.5	2.6	1.3	0.5
Current account	0.4	1.0	1.4	1.5	0.6	0.0
Private capital inflows	1.2	0.7	1.4	0.3	2.5	1.3
o/w: FDI	2.0	2.3	2.0	1.0	2.1	1.5
portfolio	-0.6	-0.7	1.0	-0.6	0.6	0.1
Public inflows	0.2	-0.4	-1.2	-0.6	0.0	0.0
Reserves/short-term-debt (%)	251	276	318	349	306	331
Reserves/monthly imports	8.2	7.3	7.0	6.8	6.9	6.7

Source: IMF staff estimates.
1/ Refers to LAC region as a whole.
2/ Projections.

Colombia, and Venezuela, is now far outpacing growth in export volumes. Furthermore, the gap between import and export volume growth is no longer expected to be offset by terms of trade improvements. Commodity prices for fuels, metals and agricultural products appear to have stabilized at high levels, and are expected to remain virtually flat on average in 2007 before declining modestly in 2008. While there continues to be great variation across countries in the level of the current account—with continuing surpluses in most commodity-exporting countries of South America, and deficits in Central America and, to a lesser extent, Mexico—the trend toward weaker current accounts is shared by most countries in the region.

Capital flows to some countries—notably Brazil, but also Argentina, Colombia, Peru, and Venezuela—increased sharply before the recent

outburst of global market volatility. Capital outflows showed a more mixed pattern, abating in Colombia and Peru, but picking up, for example, in Chile, driven by the accumulation of government assets abroad. High interest rate differentials in conjunction with appreciation pressures and limited or declining exchange rate volatility made some Latin American countries—particularly Brazil—attractive destinations for carry trades.

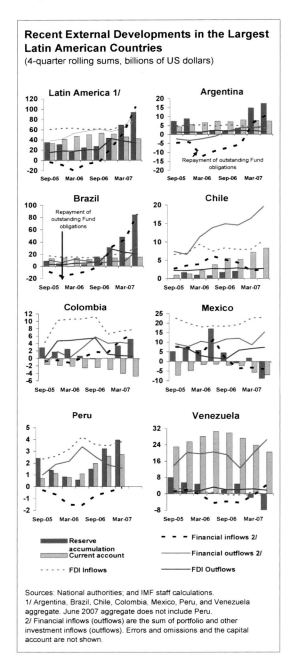

Recent External Developments in the Largest Latin American Countries
(4-quarter rolling sums, billions of US dollars)

Sources: National authorities; and IMF staff calculations.
1/ Argentina, Brazil, Chile, Colombia, Mexico, Peru, and Venezuela aggregate. June 2007 aggregate does not include Peru.
2/ Financial inflows (outflows) are the sum of portfolio and other investment inflows (outflows). Errors and omissions and the capital account are not shown.

Contribution to Changes in Trade Balance to GDP Ratios
(Percentage points, average per year)

□ Export volume effect ■ Import volume effect
□ TOT effect ▨ RER effect

Sources: WEO; and IMF staff calculations.
1/ A positive *export* effect indicates an improvement in the trade balance due to export volume growth *above* real GDP growth. A positive *import* effect indicates an improvement in the trade balance due to import volume growth *below* real GDP growth. The TOT and RER effects are the contribution from changes in terms of trade and bilateral real exchange rates (based on GDP deflators) with the United States.

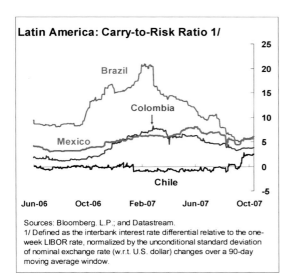

Latin America: Carry-to-Risk Ratio 1/

Sources: Bloomberg. L.P.; and Datastream.
1/ Defined as the interbank interest rate differential relative to the one-week LIBOR rate, normalized by the unconditional standard deviation of nominal exchange rate (w.r.t. U.S. dollar) changes over a 90-day moving average window.

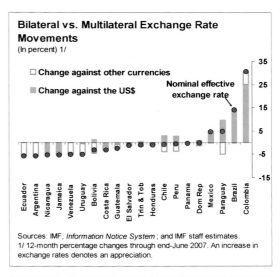

Bilateral vs. Multilateral Exchange Rate Movements
(In percent) 1/

☐ Change against other currencies
■ Change against the US$

Nominal effective exchange rate

Sources: IMF, *Information Notice System*; and IMF staff estimates.
1/ 12-month percentage changes through end-June 2007. An increase in exchange rates denotes an appreciation.

Exchange Market Pressure Index in Selected Countries 1/

Exchange market pressure index (total)

☐ Exchange rate component
■ Reserve component

Source: IMF, *International Financial Statistics*; and IMF staff calculations.
1/ The index is calculated as % change in NEER + % change in reserves * (standard deviation of % change in NEER)/(standard deviation of % change in reserves), where NEER is the nominal effective exchange rate. All percentage changes and standard deviations are computed for the 12 months between June 2006 and May 2007.

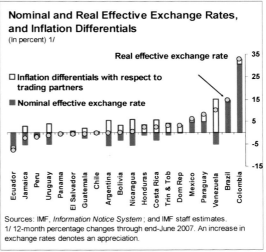

Nominal and Real Effective Exchange Rates, and Inflation Differentials
(In percent) 1/

Real effective exchange rate

☐ Inflation differentials with respect to trading partners
■ Nominal effective exchange rate

Sources: IMF, *Information Notice System*; and IMF staff estimates.
1/ 12-month percentage changes through end-June 2007. An increase in exchange rates denotes an appreciation.

Until mid-2007, surges in capital inflows and continued large current account surpluses in some commodity exporters led to significant exchange market pressures in several countries in the region. However, in only a few countries—especially Brazil and Colombia—did these pressures lead to significant bilateral appreciations against the U.S. dollar. Since the dollar has depreciated against the currencies of many other Latin American trading partners (particularly the euro zone), trade-weighted exchange rates were weaker. Indeed, nominal effective exchange rates have actually depreciated in most countries in the region this year (even before the onset of global market turbulence). At the same time, however, inflation differentials with trading partners were positive in

most cases (Ecuador and Peru were the main exceptions). The net effect of these changes was a small appreciation of the real effective exchange rate in several countries, with larger appreciations—between 10 and 35 percent in the 12 months through end-June 2007—in Colombia, Brazil, and Venezuela.

The global financial shocks in July and August 2007 initially slowed capital inflows. Central banks in several countries, including Argentina, Brazil, and Peru, reduced reserve accumulation significantly during this period compared with preceding months (in Colombia, the central bank had already stopped intervention in May). Argentina intervened in the foreign exchange

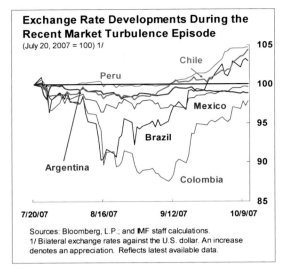

Exchange Rate Developments During the Recent Market Turbulence Episode
(July 20, 2007 = 100) 1/

Sources: Bloomberg, L.P.; and IMF staff calculations.
1/ Bilateral exchange rates against the U.S. dollar. An increase denotes an appreciation. Reflects latest available data.

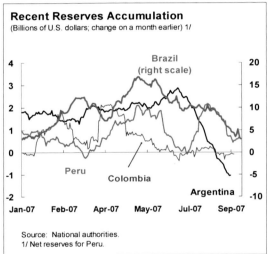

Recent Reserves Accumulation
(Billions of U.S. dollars; change on a month earlier) 1/

Source: National authorities.
1/ Net reserves for Peru.

market to lean against depreciation pressures on the currency. With the region's central banks generally much more comfortable with exchange rate fluctuation than in the past, currencies became a first shock absorber, depreciating significantly initially, although they soon began trending back to pre-turbulence levels.

FDI remains the main source of foreign capital for the region. However, it is still below the levels as a ratio to GDP reached in the late 1990s, when privatizations boosted FDI receipts for the region (Box 3). Inward FDI is now being partially offset by higher levels of outward FDI, as Latin American companies have increasingly begun to invest abroad. Following unusually low net FDI in 2006 as a result of such investments—culminating

in the US$17 billion purchase of mining assets in Canada by a Brazilian company in October 2006—net FDI inflows are projected to rebound to 1½–2 percent of GDP in 2007 and 2008.

Monetary and Exchange Rate Policies

The environment facing monetary policymakers has shifted in recent months. In the first half of 2007, monetary policy was complicated by foreign currency inflows and, in some cases, by conflicting inflation and exchange rate objectives. The recent financial turbulence and slowing external growth require a careful balance between continuing concerns about inflation and the prospect that declining external demand may slow growth and perhaps weaken price pressures in Latin America.

In the first half of 2007, buoyant cyclical conditions and incipient inflationary pressures led a number of central banks to tighten monetary policy. Interest rates were raised in four of the five countries with formal inflation targeting (Chile, Colombia, Peru, and Mexico). Several other countries—including Argentina, Bolivia, the Dominican Republic, Paraguay, and Uruguay—expanded sterilization operations to rein in rapid growth in monetary aggregates.

However, sizable foreign exchange inflows ahead of the global financial turbulence tended to overwhelm sterilization efforts, as many countries (excluding Chile and Mexico) responded to the inflows by increasing discretionary intervention in foreign exchange markets. Intervention was motivated in part by concerns about real exchange rate appreciation and eroding competitiveness (Box 4), and in part by the desire to build reserves for precautionary reasons. As a consequence, foreign exchange reserves for the region as a whole increased by almost 40 percent in the 12 months to end-June 2007, to levels that now appear comfortable from a prudential perspective (Box 5). In spite of its wide use, foreign exchange intervention has generally not been very effective in containing real appreciation in Latin America (Box 6).

Box 3. Trends in Latin America's Balance of Payments

Like other developing country regions, Latin America experienced large current account deficits during most

of the 1990s, financed by net capital inflows that helped governments fund fiscal deficits. This changed in 1998, when a "sudden stop" in private capital flows set in motion a process of rising regional current account balances and falling net capital inflows, which lasted until 2006. The Latin American experience of the past decade contrasts with that of developing Asia and— especially—Central and Eastern Europe. In Asia, current accounts also swung into surplus during the Asian crisis, but net capital flows recovered quickly, leading to large capital *and* current account inflows, and sizable reserve accumulation. In Central and Eastern Europe, current account deficits did not reverse and, in fact, continued to widen, financed by increasing net capital inflows.

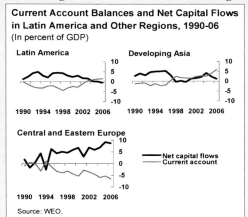

Latin America's current account reversal occurred in two phases. First, the emerging market crises of the late 1990s and the early years of this decade interrupted access of several of the largest countries to international capital markets and raised external financing costs throughout the region. Economic activity declined, fiscal adjustment took place, imports contracted, exchange rates depreciated in nominal and real terms, and exports picked up. Second, starting around 2003, import demand rose as Latin American economies began to recover, but export receipts grew more rapidly, bolstered in many countries by high commodity prices. The terms of trade improved on average by more than 20 percent between 2002 and 2006. In addition, private transfers—reflecting mainly workers' remittances— contributed to stronger current accounts in several countries, particularly in Mexico and Central America.

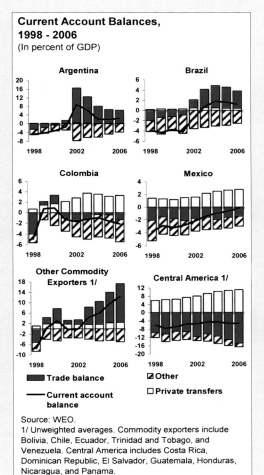

 Current account developments were not uniform across the region over the decade. Across most of South America and Mexico, external current accounts strengthened—in some cases, gradually, in others, more abruptly in response to the initial sudden stop of capital. By contrast, commodity-importing countries in Central America, which suffered terms of trade declines, continued to record large current account deficits,

---

Note: This box was prepared by Roberto Benelli.

Box 3 *(concluded)*

averaging around 5 percent of GDP, and to rely on net capital inflows (including aid) for their financing.

A decline in net capital inflows between 1998 and 2006 was accompanied by important shifts in the composition of capital flows to Latin America.[1]

- The initial decline in net flows was driven by a drop in capital inflows—particular debt and other portfolio inflows—as crises around the region made access to international capital more difficult or expensive. Inward FDI remained relatively strong, peaking in 2000 on the back of privatizations, before stabilizing at about 2½–3 percent of GDP.

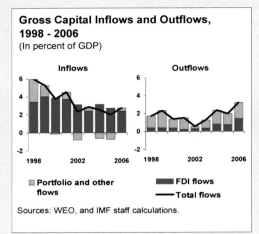

Gross Capital Inflows and Outflows, 1998 - 2006
(In percent of GDP)

Sources: WEO, and IMF staff calculations.

- In contrast, the continuing decline in net flows after 2002 is explained by a pickup in capital outflows, reflecting both higher outward FDI and higher portfolio investment abroad, in line with a worldwide trend toward greater international diversification. While gross inflows remained roughly unchanged as a share of GDP after 2002, their composition shifted, with increased lending and investment to the private sector, offset by repayments of external public debt.

As a result of the changes in both the quantity and composition of capital flows, Latin America's net foreign asset position has strengthened significantly. With external debt declining, equity liabilities growing from a low base, and foreign direct investment

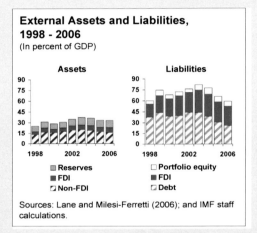

External Assets and Liabilities, 1998 - 2006
(In percent of GDP)

Sources: Lane and Milesi-Ferretti (2006); and IMF staff calculations.

liabilities broadly constant as a percentage of GDP, the region's external liabilities have fallen from over 80 percent of GDP in 2003 to around 60 percent of GDP in 2006 (on a net basis, from 40 to around 25 percent).[2] Furthermore, there has been a shift toward nondebt liabilities, and from public to private sector liabilities.

---

[1] Capital "inflows" are defined as the net purchases of domestic assets by nonresidents, and capital "outflows" as the net purchase of foreign assets by residents (with a positive sign indicating an increase in foreign assets held by domestic residents). As such, both inflows and outflows can take negative values.

[2] In spite of growing outflows (asset accumulation abroad), the value of the stock of external assets in domestic currency has declined slightly since 2003 as a result of domestic currency appreciation.

Box 4. Real Exchange Rates and Competitiveness

Real exchange rates in Latin America have generally appreciated at somewhat faster rates than in other developing countries in recent years, particularly in relation to productivity growth. Combined with high import growth and comparatively subdued export growth, this has fueled concerns among some Latin American policymakers about eroding competitiveness relative to other developing country exporters (particularly in Asia). These concerns became particularly acute during the surge in capital inflows to the region in the first half of 2007, which put significant upward pressure on some currencies.

At the same time, there is ample evidence that exchange rates in Latin America continue to be broadly in line with fundamentals. First, real exchange rates have not yet returned to their mid-1990s levels, and in most countries are hovering around their average values since 1980. Furthermore, the recent appreciation is less marked if nominal effective rates are adjusted by changes in unit labor costs (ULCs). Among the large countries, it is primarily Brazil and Colombia that have experienced effective appreciations in ULC terms, while Argentina, Chile, Peru, and Mexico have experienced broadly stable—or even declining—ULCs relative to their main trading partners. Most important, fundamentals that typically determine equilibrium exchange rates—such as net external asset positions—have significantly improved since the beginning of this decade. As a result, recent country-level studies conducted at the IMF tend to conclude that real exchange rates in the region are generally appropriately valued.

Even if Latin American exchange rates are—for the most part—well aligned with fundamentals, specific countries may be facing pressures associated with competition from abroad (e.g., China and India), particularly in third markets such as the United States (see Freund and Özden, forthcoming). However, competition in third markets does not capture the overall impact of the rapidly growing Asian economies on Latin American exports, which is positive (Lederman, Olarreaga, and Soloaga, 2007).

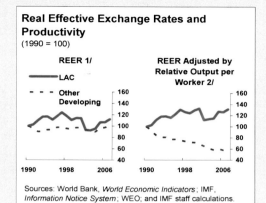

Real Effective Exchange Rates and Productivity
(1990 = 100)

Sources: World Bank, *World Economic Indicators*; IMF, *Information Notice System*; WEO; and IMF staff calculations.
1/ CPI-based REER (weighted by PPP-adjusted GDP for the countries in the grouping).
2/ The ratios of REER to country-specific indices of output per worker relative to an index of average output per worker in advanced economies.

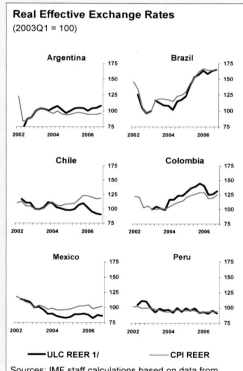

Real Effective Exchange Rates
(2003Q1 = 100)

Sources: IMF staff calculations based on data from national authorities; and IMF, *International Financial Statistics*.
1/ ULC REER based on aggregate economy, or manufacturing when aggregate economy not available.

Note: This box was prepared by Roberto Benelli and Jeromin Zettelmeyer.

Box 5. Optimal Prudential Reserve Levels

Recent reserves accumulation in Latin America has often been motivated by the desire to acquire a "cushion" that would protect the economy and smooth consumption in the event of a sudden stop in capital flows. However, maintaining liquid reserves also imposes quasi-fiscal costs. What level of reserves is optimal in light of these benefits and costs? In a recent IMF working paper, Olivier Jeanne and Romain Rancière (2006) answer this question in a simple utility-maximizing framework.[1] The result is a formula for the optimal level of reserves from a prudential perspective that states that optimal reserves should be larger: (1) the larger the size and output cost of a crisis (the "sudden stop" of capital inflows that the country wishes to protect itself from); (2) the higher the probability of the sudden stop and (3) the lower the cost of holding reserves. The latter is typically calibrated as the average spread between 10-year U.S. treasury bonds and the federal funds rate, while the output cost is based on past crises experiences. The need for foreign currency in a sudden stop depends on short-term debt, and foreign currency deposits net of banks' liquid foreign assets (Gonçalves, forthcoming).

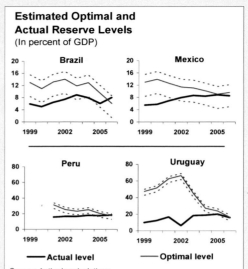

Estimated Optimal and Actual Reserve Levels
(In percent of GDP)

Source: Author's calculations.
Note: The baseline optimal level of reserves is based on illustrative parameter values, including a probability of a sudden stop of capital inflows of 10 percent, a term premium of 1.5 percent, and a risk-aversion parameter of 2. The need for reserves and output loss are calibrated as in the original studies. The dashed lines indicate the range for the optimal level of reserves when the probability of a sudden stop varies between 5 and 20 percent.

IMF staff have separately applied Jeanne and Rancière's formula to Mexico, Brazil, Peru, and Uruguay, using country-specific information to calibrate foreign exchange needs in a crisis and the likely output cost if a crisis occurs. Despite these differences, all four studies reached a similar conclusion: the gap between the optimal and actual reserve levels appears to have closed in recent years. The figure illustrates this general finding by making common assumptions (for country comparison purposes only) about the likelihood of a sudden stop, the cost of holding reserves, and the risk-aversion parameter.

The figure shows that the closing gap results from both reserve accumulation and falling optimal reserve levels as measured by Jeanne and Rancière's formula. The fall in optimal reserve levels reflects declining short-term debt and net foreign currency deposits in recent years. As vulnerabilities have decreased, so has the optimal level of reserves calculated to be needed to self-insure against a "sudden stop."

While optimal reserves estimates are notably sensitive to the crisis likelihood parameter (as shown by the dashed lines in the figure), the studies suggest that reserves have now approached comfortable levels. Nonetheless, a key message of the model is that the optimal level of reserves can rapidly increase if vulnerabilities return to past levels, warranting caution about future short-term foreign currency debt issuance and/or future increases in net foreign currency deposits.

Note: This box was prepared by Fernando M. Gonçalves.

[1] See also related work by Mulder and Bussière (1999); IMF (2000, 2001); Garcia and Soto (2006); and Jeanne (2007). The latter two studies go beyond the mitigating role of reserves and consider that reserves may also help prevent crises.

Box 6. Effectiveness of Central Bank Intervention—Evidence from Colombia

How effective is central bank intervention in influencing the nominal exchange rate? While there is an extensive literature on this subject for advanced economies, less is known about the effectiveness of intervention as an independent policy tool in emerging markets.[1] A major hurdle has been the lack of official, high-frequency data on central bank intervention (because of valuation changes, this cannot be inferred simply from changes in reserves). Moreover, it is often not possible to know, for example, whether authorities accumulate reserves with the intent of affecting the exchange rate or for other reasons, such as, self-insurance against external financial shocks.

Drawing on a new dataset on daily official statistics on foreign exchange intervention by the central bank of Colombia (Banco de la República), a recent study by Kamil (2007) examines the impact of discretionary intervention on the level and volatility of the nominal spot exchange rate in Colombia over the period September 2004 to April 2007. The case of Colombia is of particular interest for three reasons. First, Colombia has faced strong exchange rate appreciation pressures. Second, the period under study was punctuated by frequent, and at times large, discretionary purchases of foreign exchange to resist domestic currency appreciation. During these periods, intervention took place on almost 80 percent of business days. As a result, between January 2004 and May 2007, reserves almost doubled (from US$10.5 billion to approximately US$20 billion). Third, as shown in the first panel of the figure, the sample period considered in the study spans two distinctly different regimes with respect to the stance of monetary policy: one characterized by constant or falling interest rates (September 2004 to March 2006), and a second one by a tightening of monetary policy and an increase in nominal interest rates to reduce inflationary pressures (January to April 2007). This provides an opportunity to test the hypothesis that discretionary intervention to stem domestic currency appreciation is more effective when there is consistency between monetary and exchange rate policy goals.

Estimation results indicate that the effects of Banco de la República intervention varied sharply across the two periods. During the first period of unannounced, discretionary intervention (December 2004–March 2006), Banco de la República foreign currency purchases had a statistically significant, positive impact on the exchange rate level. However, while discretionary intervention contributed toward moderating the appreciation trend, its effect was economically small and short lived. For example, a US$30 million sterilized purchase of foreign exchange (the average daily amount of intervention within this period) would depreciate the value of the domestic currency by 0.32 percent. Further, intervention operations did not have a lasting impact on exchange rate dynamics: almost 70 percent of the contemporaneous effect was reversed in two days. Controlling for other factors affecting short-term exchange rate volatility, results also indicate that central bank intervention dampened the volatility of exchange rate returns during this period.

During the second period (January–April 2007), Banco de la República intervention did not influence the level of the exchange rate, even in the short term. Banco de la República's intervention operations aimed at depreciating the currency were drowned out by offsetting movements in the EMBI spread and market reactions to higher-than-expected GDP and inflation announcements. During this period, there was a tension between monetary and exchange rate policy goals, as markets perceived that the policy of large-scale foreign currency purchases was not consistent with meeting the Banco de la República's inflation

Note: This box was prepared by Herman Kamil.

[1] Recent contributions using daily data for emerging markets include Guimarães and Karacadag (2004) for Turkey and Mexico and Disyatat and Galati (2007) for the Czech Republic. Canales-Kriljenko (2003) provides a summary of central bank intervention practices in developing countries.

Box 6 *(concluded)*

target (see second panel of figure). To stem the appreciation of the peso, the Banco de la República intervened aggressively, accumulating US$4.5 billion (38 percent of monetary base) in the first four months of 2007. At the same time, to cope with inflation pressures, it steadily increased its policy interest rate. But this had the consequence of attracting more capital inflows, thereby exacerbating appreciation pressures.

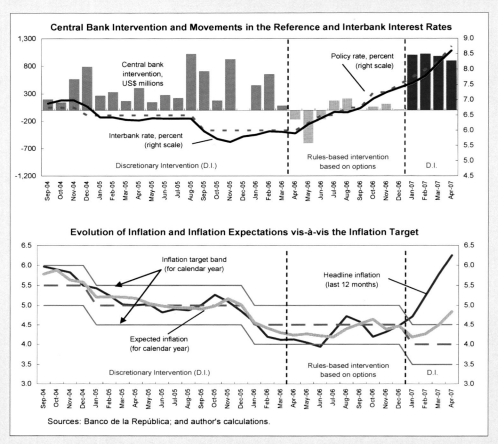

Sources: Banco de la República; and author's calculations.

 This tension between foreign exchange purchases and interest rate hikes opened the door to adverse market dynamics and one-way bets against the Banco de la República, which manifested itself in two ways. First, offshore entities built large long positions in pesos through the onshore forward market, as Colombia—with nominal interest rates 800 basis points above Japan's—became one focal point for carry trade in Latin America. Second, consistent with Toro and Julio (2006), results indicate that trading volumes on the spot FX market increased abnormally on days when the Banco de la República intervened, even after correcting for changes in volatility and other macroeconomic factors. The Banco de la República decided to stop intervention in May, noting that continued intervention would have compromised achieving its inflation target (Banco de la República, 2007).

In sum, the results suggest that coherence between the intervention policy and inflation objectives is a critical factor in determining the success of discretionary intervention. While a government committed to resisting appreciation in principle has an unlimited supply of "ammunition," inflation objectives can become a binding constraint.

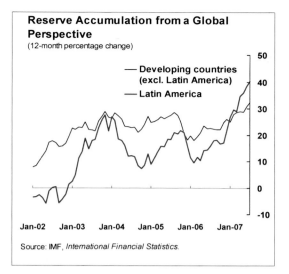

Reserve Accumulation from a Global Perspective
(12-month percentage change)

— Developing countries (excl. Latin America)
— Latin America

Source: IMF, *International Financial Statistics.*

Some countries went beyond intervention in attempting to reduce real appreciation pressures or offset their effect on competitiveness. Colombia established an unremunerated reserve requirement (URR) of 40 percent on external borrowing and gross portfolio inflows for six months (a similar URR has existed in Argentina since 2005). At the same time, it set tighter prudential limits on forward currency operations. Other actions comprised extensive administrative measures to contain inflation in Argentina, including limiting price adjustments in regulated industries, selective price agreements, and export restraints; and import tariffs and/or subsidized credit lines to help domestic producers deal with low-cost competition from abroad in Brazil and Colombia (the latter measures have so far remained small in scale).

Following the financial turbulence in industrialized markets, the main challenge facing monetary authorities in the region has shifted to assessing the impact of the deteriorating external environment against the backdrop of continued inflationary pressures in a number of countries. Although most economies in the region are operating at or above capacity—in itself a source of inflation pressure—a significant drop in U.S. economic growth could lead to slower growth in the region. In addition, central banks need to decide whether and how to react to rising food prices, which are likely to reflect international

conditions in food markets—and thus a relative price adjustment—but could also be a sign of rapid domestic demand growth and cyclical conditions.

As central banks have weighed these trade-offs and individual country circumstances, monetary policy in the region has been cautiously tightened in some countries and put on hold in others. Notably, Chile and Peru raised rates in September and Mexico did so in late October, but Chile left rates on hold during its October policy meeting. Brazil continued its stepwise reduction of interest rates through early September but has since left rates unchanged.

Fiscal Policy

Primary fiscal surpluses—a key source of recent strength in the region—peaked in 2006 and are projected to decline to about 2 percent in 2007 and 1¾ percent in 2008, as revenue ratios stabilize or fall at a time when expenditure is still growing rapidly. Structural (cyclically adjusted) primary balances generally appear to remain in surplus. However, they are lower than current reported surpluses, and there is significant uncertainty about their size, particularly in the case of commodity exporters.

Primary fiscal surpluses in Latin America appear to have peaked in 2006 after strengthening for several years during which revenue growth

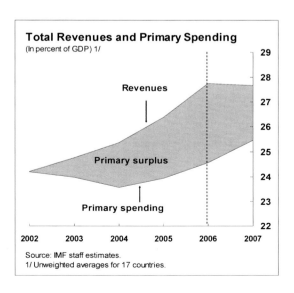

Total Revenues and Primary Spending
(In percent of GDP) 1/

Revenues

Primary surplus

Primary spending

Source: IMF staff estimates.
1/ Unweighted averages for 17 countries.

outpaced rising expenditures. In 2007, expenditure has continued to grow rapidly—at a projected 9 percent in real terms on average—or faster than real GDP. But revenue-to-GDP ratios are projected to decline slightly, mainly as a result of flat or slightly lower commodity prices and/or production. As a result, primary surpluses will shrink this year to an expected regional average of about 2 percent of GDP, although with significant outliers. These include Chile, where the primary balance is projected to remain over 7 percent of GDP in line with the structural surplus rule, and Venezuela, where high real spending growth in 2006 and a decline in oil revenue as share of GDP could push the 2007 primary balance into negative territory for the first time in six years.

In light of this, it is important to assess how strong underlying fiscal positions are in Latin America. Are "structural" primary balances still in surplus? And how rapidly will they turn to deficits if spending growth continues unabated? These questions are addressed in Chapter 4, which analyzes the sources of revenue growth since 2002 and estimates how far primary balances would shrink simply as a result of a return to a neutral position in the economic cycle, and of the likely level of commodity revenues over the medium term. The main results are as follows:

- Increases in commodity revenues have played an important role in the recent rise of revenues in the main commodity-exporting countries. These have been driven mostly by higher commodity prices, but also by increases in royalties and commodity-related taxes and, in some cases, by increases in production volumes.

- In contrast, country business cycles have had only small identifiable effects on revenue ratios. In most countries, noncommodity revenues tend to rise roughly in proportion to economic activity, leaving the ratio to GDP approximately unchanged.

- Tax policy has played a significant role in raising revenue in some countries—notably Brazil and El Salvador—while tax administration changes helped raise the revenue ratio in Costa Rica.

- Finally, in some countries, including Argentina, Colombia, and Panama, revenues as a share of GDP have increased by more than can be clearly explained by these factors. A few other countries have had analogous unexplained declines in noncommodity revenue rates. In some, but not all, of these cases, the causes of these "residual" changes can be identified upon closer inspection of each country case.

Hence, the strength of Latin America's underlying revenue positions today depends importantly on whether increases in commodity prices, as well as recent "residual" surges in noncommodity revenues are temporary or permanent. Although there is significant uncertainty in both dimensions, the analysis supports a general conclusion: structural primary surpluses are more modest than the unadjusted data indicate, particularly in commodity-exporting countries facing possible declines in prices over the medium term (see Chapter 4 for details).

At the same time, fiscal policy remains expansionary. As expenditure growth continues to outpace both revenue and GDP growth in many countries, fiscal surpluses—both actual and structural—are shrinking fast. In oil-exporting

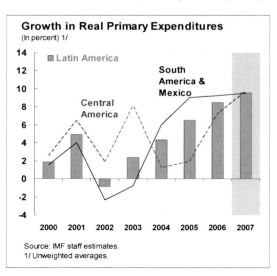

Growth in Real Primary Expenditures
(In percent) 1/

Source: IMF staff estimates.
1/ Unweighted averages.

countries, in particular, noncommodity primary balances are worsening.[1] Unless spending growth is curbed, many countries in the region are likely to return to structural deficits in 2008.

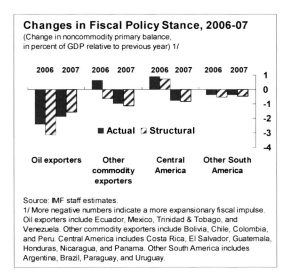

Changes in Fiscal Policy Stance, 2006-07
(Change in noncommodity primary balance, in percent of GDP relative to previous year) 1/

Source: IMF staff estimates.
1/ More negative numbers indicate a more expansionary fiscal impulse. Oil exporters include Ecuador, Mexico, Trinidad & Tobago, and Venezuela. Other commodity exporters include Bolivia, Chile, Colombia, and Peru. Central America includes Costa Rica, El Salvador, Guatemala, Honduras, Nicaragua, and Panama. Other South America includes Argentina, Brazil, Paraguay, and Uruguay.

In the last 12 months, a number of countries have initiated fiscal reforms, focused mostly on the tax system.[2] Peru undertook several reforms aimed at broadening the tax base—particularly by rationalizing tax incentives—and lowering distortionary taxes, including through the stepwise reduction of the financial transactions tax. Colombia and Uruguay adopted broadly revenue-neutral tax reforms aimed at enhancing efficiency and also—in the case of Uruguay—at making the tax system more equitable, including by

---

[1] Changes in noncommodity primary balances—that is, changes in primary balances minus changes in commodity revenues—are a better indicator of fiscal contractions or expansions than primary balances per se, because changes in commodity revenue are mostly driven by payments by nonresidents, and as such do not have the usual direct impact on domestic disposable income (see the November 2006 *Regional Economic Outlook: Western Hemisphere*).

[2] Several countries also initiated or completed changes to their pension systems. In Chile and Mexico, these reforms were aimed mainly at boosting competition among private pension fund administrators, and, in the case of Chile, at widening coverage. In Argentina, the government widened the scope of the public system, including by moving government employees and allowing other workers to switch to the public system.

introducing a personal income tax. Mexico passed a fiscal reform package that includes a new minimum tax, improvements in expenditure management and revenue administration, and changes in intergovernmental fiscal relations. This is expected to raise about 2 percent of GDP over the next few years, to help cover declining oil revenues and new infrastructure spending. In Brazil, the authorities have announced plans for a comprehensive reform of the indirect tax system, merging all consumption taxes into two value-added taxes (a federal and a state-level VAT), and aiming for a significant simplification in tax administration. Several Caribbean countries—Antigua and Barbuda, Dominica, Guyana, and St. Vincent and the Grenadines—have also embarked on tax modernization initiatives, including the implementation of VAT systems.

As a result of strong growth, some real appreciation, and continuing (albeit smaller) primary surpluses, public debt levels have continued their decline in 2006 and 2007, to about 50 percent of GDP in Latin America on a GDP-weighted basis and just under 40 percent on an unweighted basis (projections for end-2007). However, debt ratios remain above mid-1990s lows in several Latin American countries including Argentina, Brazil, Colombia, and Uruguay, and in the region as a whole on a weighted average basis. As discussed previously (see in particular, the November 2006 *Regional Economic Outlook: Western Hemisphere*, Box 1), debt structures have also

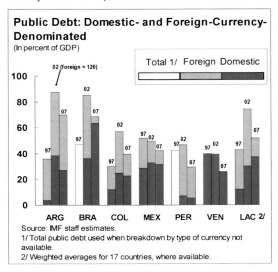

Public Debt: Domestic- and Foreign-Currency-Denominated
(In percent of GDP)

Source: IMF staff estimates.
1/ Total public debt used when breakdown by type of currency not available.
2/ Weighted averages for 17 countries, where available.

improved across the board, with much less reliance on foreign currency debt and lengthening of local currency maturities. This trend has continued in 2007, with several countries— including Brazil, Chile, Mexico, and Peru—issuing long-term bonds in local currency, including in international markets.

Social Policies

Poverty continues to decline but inequality remains high in the region. To tackle persistent inequality and high poverty, better targeting of social spending is essential.

There has been significant progress in reducing both extreme and total poverty rates in Latin America in recent years—the latter to around 38 percent of the population in 2006.[3] Recent national data show a particularly impressive decline in Argentina, where the poverty rate has fallen by over 30 percentage points since 2002, reversing a large rise during the crisis period between 1999 and 2002. Brazil and Colombia have also achieved significant reductions—7½ and 10½ percentage points, respectively—since 2002. However, large differences in poverty levels remain across countries. In Chile, the percentage of the population below the national poverty line is below 14 percent, while it is in the 20–30 percent range in Argentina, Brazil, Costa Rica, Mexico, and Uruguay; around 40 percent in Peru; and over 50 percent in Bolivia.[4] Income inequality, while persistent, has also decreased in most countries in the region since the late 1990s. Latin American countries still tend to have much higher inequality than countries of similar levels of

[3] Projections by the Economic Commission for Latin America and the Caribbean (ECLAC) show a decline in the overall poverty rate.

[4] National poverty lines are not strictly comparable across countries, but an attempt was made to choose similar definitions when multiple definitions were available in a country. Using internationally comparable poverty headcount ratios (percentage of the population who live under $2 a day) leads to a broadly similar country ranking. Unfortunately, headcount ratios are not available after 2004; gauging recent trends hence requires the use of national data.

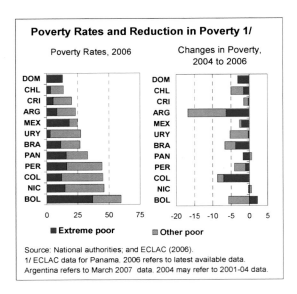

Poverty Rates and Reduction in Poverty 1/

Poverty Rates, 2006 — Changes in Poverty, 2004 to 2006

■ Extreme poor   ■ Other poor

Source: National authorities; and ECLAC (2006).
1/ ECLAC data for Panama. 2006 refers to latest available data. Argentina refers to March 2007 data. 2004 may refer to 2001-04 data.

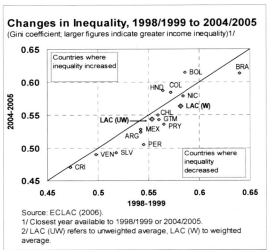

Changes in Inequality, 1998/1999 to 2004/2005
(Gini coefficient; larger figures indicate greater income inequality)1/

Source: ECLAC (2006).
1/ Closest year available to 1998/1999 or 2004/2005.
2/ LAC (UW) refers to unweighted average, LAC (W) to weighted average.

development in Asia and Europe, possibly dampening the potential effect of economic growth on reducing poverty (see Box 7, and the October 2007 *World Economic Outlook*, Chapter 4). Furthermore, trend growth continues to be weaker in Latin America than in other developing country regions, particularly when the favorable external environment of recent years is taken into account.

As the expansion has consolidated, social spending has continued to rise. With greater macroeconomic stability, these outlays have also become less volatile. However, the region still has

Box 7. Escaping Poverty in Latin America

Robust economic growth has helped to reduce poverty significantly in Latin America in recent years, reflecting both the strength of the expansion, by historical standards, and a greater impact of growth on poverty. Argentina has experienced the largest poverty decline, followed by Bolivia, Brazil, Chile, Colombia, Mexico, Peru, and Uruguay. Countries with low growth have experienced less impressive declines in poverty. Based on these recent national estimates, on average, a 1 percentage point increase in growth has corresponded to a 1.7 percent reduction in poverty in Latin America between 2002 and 2006 (population weighted). Similarly, studies using household surveys find that the poverty response to growth was about 1.2 percent between 2002 and 2005 (ECLAC, 2006). This is more than twice as high as during

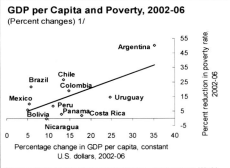

GDP per Capita and Poverty, 2002-06
(Percent changes) 1/

Sources: National authorities; ECLAC (2006); and World Bank, *World Development Indicators*.
1/ Poverty rate defined as percentage of population below national poverty line. Latest period corresponding to poverty data availability. For Chile and Uruguay refers to 2003-06; for Mexico and Bolivia refers to 2002-05; for Peru refers to 2004-06.

the 1990s, when a 1 percentage point increase in growth reduced poverty by only 0.6 percent on average. And, unlike in the 1990s, economic growth has tended to go along with lower income inequality. Hence, poverty reductions seem to have resulted from a combination of both higher growth and distribution improvements.

Why has recent growth been comparatively pro-poor and distribution-friendly? While it is hard to answer this question comprehensively, recent experience provides some clues. In contrast with earlier episodes, the current expansion has seen a significant reduction in unemployment rates across the region (see the April 2007 *Regional Economic Outlook: Western Hemisphere*, Box 6; and Loayza and Raddatz, 2006). There have also been improvements in the targeting of social spending, including through the creation of conditional cash transfer programs in countries such as Argentina, Brazil, Mexico, Chile, Colombia, and Uruguay. Chile's success in halving poverty between 1990 and 1998, for example, has been attributed to a combination of growth and well-targeted social programs (World Bank, 2001); and recent studies of the impact of conditional cash transfer programs have shown that these transfers are better targeted than most social spending and contribute significantly to poverty reduction (Perry and others, 2006). Finally, workers' remittances to Latin American countries have risen significantly in recent years. By effectively providing privately funded social safety nets and helping finance household investment and education, remittances could also have played a role in reducing poverty (Fajnzylber and López, 2007).

In spite of the recent successes, poverty in the region remains high, at about 38 percent in 2006. Further reduction will depend first and foremost on sustaining the current economic expansion while containing inflation, and thus breaking decisively with Latin America's tradition of macroeconomic volatility. Moreover, poverty remains stubbornly high within particular socioeconomic groups. Indigenous peoples and female-headed households continue to be at the bottom of the income distribution. Countries with high rural populations face additional challenges as poverty is both much higher and less responsive to growth

---

Note: This box was prepared by Priya Joshi.

Box 7 (concluded)

in rural than in urban regions. Finally, urban poverty, while comparatively low, has been rising in some countries. Measures that could help address these challenges include:

- a greater effort to reach the rural poor, including through better service delivery to rural areas, tackling land inequality, improving rural infrastructure (Perry and others, 2006; Echeverría, 2000; López and Valdés, 2000);

- better quality of primary and secondary education especially in rural areas (de Ferranti and others, 2003; Vegas and Petrow, 2007);

- removal of barriers to private investment, particularly in employment-intensive industries such as in the agricultural sector (de Ferranti and others, 2005); and

- labor market reforms to reduce incentives for employment in the informal sector, in which workers tend to be lower paid and lack benefits such as health insurance and social security (ECLAC, 2006).

---

considerable scope to improve the efficiency of social spending; the quality of primary education, for example, continues to lag behind other regions of the world (Vegas and Petrow, 2007). And social spending continues to benefit primarily middle- and upper-income groups rather than the poor, owing to the high share of these outlays absorbed by higher education and social insurance. Indeed, social spending in many countries in the region has been regressive, benefiting the richer segments of society more than the poor in absolute terms.

Social spending may nonetheless reduce measured inequality in Latin America, because the poor's share of the benefits from social spending tends to be larger than their share of pre-transfer income. As shown in a new study by IMF staff (Cubero and Vladkova-Hollar, forthcoming), this effect is generally positive although small (particularly in light of the high degree of inequality of the pre–fiscal policy income distribution). In Central America, for example, the combined redistributive effect of taxation and social spending has been to reduce the Gini coefficient by around 4.5 percentage points on average, with large variations—from 1.6 percentage points in El Salvador to 8 percentage points in Panama.

Targeted social assistance programs, which combine transfers to the poor with health or education-related goals, hold some promise for reducing poverty. Recent evaluations of the

conditional cash transfer program *Oportunidades* in Mexico have demonstrated that the poverty alleviation potential of such programs can lead to improved health and education, as well as more

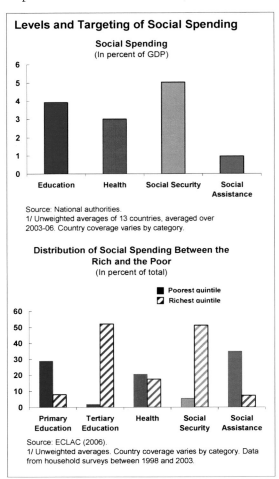

Levels and Targeting of Social Spending

Social Spending
(In percent of GDP)

Source: National authorities.
1/ Unweighted averages of 13 countries, averaged over 2003-06. Country coverage varies by category.

Distribution of Social Spending Between the Rich and the Poor
(In percent of total)

Source: ECLAC (2006).
1/ Unweighted averages. Country coverage varies by category. Data from household surveys between 1998 and 2003.

capacity for investments, as credit constraints of poor beneficiaries are eased (Gertler, Martinez, and Rubio-Codina, 2007; Freije, Bando, and Arce, 2007). The *Chile Solidario* program, a social protection system that targets the poorest families, has been important in helping lower Chilean poverty rates from 19 percent in 2002 to below 14 percent in 2006. Programs of this type have also been implemented in other countries, including Argentina, Panama, Peru, and Brazil— where the *Bolsa Família* program has been expanded rapidly in the last four years to reach almost 12 million households. Other related social policy initiatives have also recently taken place in Peru—with a new national strategy to combat malnutrition among young children—Uruguay, and Nicaragua, which has launched a new social safety net program (*Hambre Cero*).

III. How Resilient Is Latin America's Expansion?

A striking fact of Latin America's economic history is the frequency and regularity with which growth, once under way, has suffered setbacks. Expansions have often been short lived, ending with crises or prolonged periods of stagnation. Latin American business cycles have tended to be volatile compared with those of both advanced countries and other developing countries (Aiolfi, Catão, and Timmerman, 2006). Long-run growth spells—sustained periods of growth, with only transitory interruptions—have tended to be rarer (Berg, Ostry, and Zettelmeyer, forthcoming). Finally, large output drops have happened more frequently in Latin America than in any other region except for Africa (Becker and Mauro, 2006). Previous issues of this *Regional Economic Outlook* argued that improvements in Latin American macroeconomic fundamentals since the beginning of this decade, coupled with reforms initiated in the 1980s and 1990s, justified hopes that the current economic expansion could be more sustained than its predecessors.

The recent global financial turbulence, and slowing growth in the United States and other industrial countries, constitute Latin America's first real test of resilience to external shocks since 2002. How will the region's expansion, now in its fifth year, react to these shocks? This chapter examines the potential channels of transmission of foreign shocks, and analyzes Latin America's outlook in the context of a deteriorating external environment, using econometric techniques. It concludes that, based on current WEO projections for external growth, commodity prices, and international credit market conditions, the Latin American expansion is likely to continue, albeit at a somewhat slower pace. However, there are significant risks. These relate, in particular, to variations in the strength of fundamentals within the region, fluctuations in U.S. growth—to which some countries in the region remain highly sensitive, especially in Central America and

Mexico—and the possibility that the financial turbulence may widen or deepen, with repercussions for global growth and commodity prices.

Channels of Transmission

Tighter external financing conditions have in the past played a key role in financial crises and output collapses in Latin America. During the 1990s and in the early years of this decade, sudden stops in capital inflows have triggered currency crises, which created widespread insolvencies, as public and private sector liabilities were often denominated in U.S. dollars. This in turn set off bank runs, sharp credit crunches, and, in a few cases, a collapse of the entire financial system. In some cases monetary authorities were able to avoid sharp depreciations, but this came at the price of very high interest rates, taking a significant toll on growth.

In principle, the latest turbulence in world financial markets and its repercussions on the global economy could affect Latin America through four channels: (1) real external demand, as growth in trading partners—particularly the United States—is adversely affected; (2) declines in commodity prices and the terms of trade as a result of a deceleration in world economic activity; (3) financial channels, including through a higher cost of capital and a reduction or reversal in capital flows to the region; and finally (4) a decline in private remittances to the region, as incomes and credit of Latin American workers abroad, particularly in the United States, are reduced. Furthermore, domestic policy reactions can play a role in either mitigating or exacerbating external shocks. In the past, the first three transmission channels have played important roles in precipitating crises in Latin America, while procyclical fiscal policies and monetary policies (for example, in an attempt to reduce unfinanced deficits or defend an exchange rate level) have amplified the shock. To what extent is each likely to be relevant this time? And is there a significant role for remittances as a new channel of transmission, as a recent slowdown in remittances to Central America and Mexico, coinciding with the collapse of new housing construction in the United States, may suggest?

"Current account channels"—export demand and remittances—are surely relevant; but the strength of their effect will depend on the extent to which economic activity slows in trade partner countries. In turn, this will likely depend on the prospects for the U.S. economy. A recent IMF study (the April 2007 *World Economic Outlook*, Chapter 4) suggests that a "midcycle slowdown" in the United States—as opposed to a full-blown recession—would not significantly affect world growth, particularly given robust growth in emerging markets. Furthermore, Latin America as a whole has become less dependent on U.S. demand. Exports to the United States have declined from 57 percent of total exports in 2000 to 47 percent in 2006—although they remain very high for Mexico (85 percent) and some Central American countries. Finally, while remittances to Latin America have until recently been on a fast-rising trend, their magnitude as a share of GDP remains fairly modest, although not in Central American and some Caribbean countries. A recent IMF study shows that remittances to Latin America have in the past not been strongly influenced by the U.S. economic cycle (Box 8). However, past patterns may not be a particularly good guide to the future. This is in part due to the role of the weaker housing market in the United States in the recent turbulence, and the importance of the U.S. housing and construction sectors as an area of employment and—increasingly—investment for immigrants from the region.

Similarly, a significant reduction in commodity prices would surely affect the region. Estimates in the April 2007 *Regional Economic Outlook* suggested that a decline in relevant commodity export prices

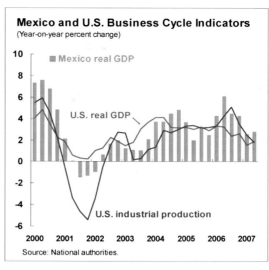

Mexico and U.S. Business Cycle Indicators
(Year-on-year percent change)

Source: National authorities.

Size of Remittances in Latin America, 2006

	Billions of US$	Percent of	
		GDP	FDI inflows
South America			
Brazil	2.9	0.3	15.4
Chile	-1.8	1.2	20.5
Colombia	3.9	2.9	61.8
Ecuador	2.9	7.2	100.6
Mexico	23.7	2.7	102.8
Peru	1.8	2.0	50.5
Central America			
Costa Rica	0.5	2.3	73.8
El Salvador	3.3	18.1	667.3
Guatemala	3.6	10.2	1110.7
Honduras	2.2	25.0	774.2
Nicaragua	0.7	12.2	235.3
Dominican Republic	2.7	8.7	324.7

Sources: National authorities; IMF, *International Financial Statistics*; and IMF staff calculations.

by 5 percent in one quarter would reduce aggregate growth in six large Latin American economies (Argentina, Brazil, Chile, Colombia, Mexico and Peru) by about one-third of a percentage point after two quarters. However, the relevant prices of goods exported by Latin American countries continue to be high, with only mild declines currently projected over the medium term. A significantly larger decline is likely only in the context of a sharp downturn in world growth, examined in the next section.

Box 8. Are Remittances to Latin America Influenced by the U.S. Business Cycle?

While there is evidence that remittances may help to smooth adverse home country shocks, little is known about the potential impact on remittances of shocks in the source country. Experience in the first half of 2007, when a remittance slowdown to some Latin American countries coincided with a moderating U.S. economy, suggested a procyclical link (see first figure). However, a closer analysis of the data suggests that such links remain weak.

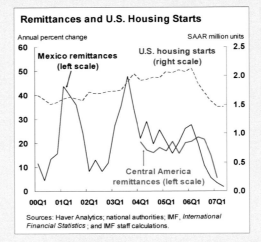

Remittances and U.S. Housing Starts

Sources: Haver Analytics; national authorities; IMF, *International Financial Statistics*; and IMF staff calculations.

In a recent IMF study, Roache and Gradzka (forthcoming) examine the link between remittances to 15 Latin American countries, using quarterly data between 1994 and 2007 and 19 indicators of the U.S. business cycle, using a range of methods. Simple correlations between seasonally adjusted and deflated remittances and U.S. cyclical indicators, averaged

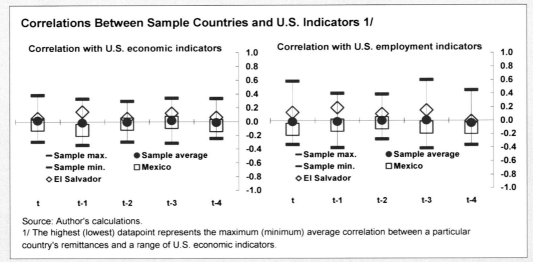

Correlations Between Sample Countries and U.S. Indicators 1/

Source: Author's calculations.
1/ The highest (lowest) datapoint represents the maximum (minimum) average correlation between a particular country's remittances and a range of U.S. economic indicators.

across countries and indicators, turn out to be close to zero (left panel of second figure). Similar results were obtained using more narrowly defined groups of U.S. indicators, such as employment growth, and lagging the U.S. indicators by 1 to 4 quarters (right panel of second figure). In addition to averages, the figure shows individually the correlations for Mexico as the largest recipient of remittance (in absolute terms, not in relation to GDP), and El Salvador, the country with the highest average correlation.

Regressing remittances on a range of U.S. indicators, with lags and controlling for the domestic business cycle, also failed to detect a clear and positive relationship in most cases. In a final step, one can ask whether it is possible to detect a "common cycle" among U.S. economic activity and remittance flows. To do this, a "dynamic factor analysis" was undertaken for the six countries with the most data and four U.S. business cycle indicators, including GDP, two employment measures, and housing starts (see table). The more positive the coefficients in the table, the more sensitive are remittances to the U.S. cycle. The results again

Note: This box was prepared by Shaun Roache.

Box 8 *(concluded)*

suggest little or no sensitivity for most countries. Mexico may be an exception, as remittances to Mexico appear related to a broad measure of the U.S. economic cycle; indeed, recent data for Mexico continue to suggest an emerging linkage (see Roache and Gradzka, forthcoming, for details)

It is possible that stronger linkages will emerge, as the rapid pace of recorded remittance growth begins to

Dynamic Common Factor Model: Sensitivity of Remittances 1/

Factor	Argentina	Brazil	Dominican Republic	El Salvador	Guatemala	Mexico	U.S. GDP	U.S. employment in: construction	U.S. employment in: services
	Hodrick-Prescott cyclical component model - estimated factor loadings								
U.S. cycle	-0.13	-0.10	-0.06	0.09	0.14	0.66*	0.29***	0.32***	0.24***
	[0.58]	[0.68]	[0.58]	[0.48]	[0.34]	[0.35]	[0.06]	[0.05]	[0.06]
Remittances	0.55**	0.67**	0.31	-0.33	0.32	-0.02	...	...	...
	[0.22]	[0.30]	[0.49]	[0.57]	[0.42]	[0.33]	...	...	...

Source: Roache and Gradzka (forthcoming)
1/ The coefficients are the factor loadings (or sensitivity) of each variable in the observable vector to the unobservable factors which represent the U.S. cycle and a common remittance effect. These results were based on estimations using the cyclical component of the Hodrick-Prescott filter. Significance at 1, 5, and 10 percent levels indicated by ***, **, and *, respectively. Coefficient standard errors are in brackets.

slow. However, it is also possible that migrants may engage in a form of consumption smoothing by sending home a fixed amount each month; this has also been proposed as a possible reason for the countercyclical response of remittances to conditions in the home country (see Sayan, 2006).

Financial vulnerabilities are reduced compared with a few years ago, although they have not disappeared. Currency mismatches associated with foreign currency borrowing have come down in several countries, and external positions are generally stronger (see Box 3). Fiscal positions

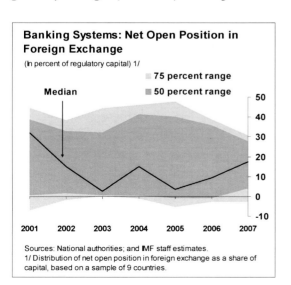

Banking Systems: Net Open Position in Foreign Exchange
(In percent of regulatory capital) 1/

- 75 percent range
- 50 percent range
- Median

Sources: National authorities; and IMF staff estimates.
1/ Distribution of net open position in foreign exchange as a share of capital, based on a sample of 9 countries.

have also improved, and structural primary balances are generally in surplus (see Chapter 4). Public sector financing requirements are generally lower, with maturing public debt in 2007 below 10 percent of GDP in most large countries. There is also little indication of direct exposure of Latin American banks to the U.S. subprime market or a clear cause for concern over domestic bank solvency at this stage (Box 9). However, both fiscal and external positions in the region are expected to deteriorate this year, and recent rapid credit growth may have led to financial sector vulnerabilities that are not yet visible.

Corporate health among larger companies has also improved. Comparing the period of 2002–06 with that of 1998–2001, the publicly listed firms in the region have generated higher earnings, become more liquid, and face lower gross rollover risks. These improvements mean that the corporate sector—at least, publicly listed firms—may be in a stronger position than before to cope with adverse

Box 9. Will the U.S. Subprime Crisis Affect Bank Lending in Latin America?

There is little indication of *direct* exposure of Latin American banks to the U.S. subprime market, or clear cause for concern over bank solvency. Market-based default estimates for publicly listed financial institutions in the region have stayed low in absolute terms and below their historic values. The aggregate liquidity condition of the banking systems in the larger Latin American countries in the first part of 2007 was generally strong, providing some buffer for the subsequent turmoil in the global financial markets. There was little sign of liquidity problems in reaction to the turbulence (a brief spike in interbank rates in Argentina was addressed by central bank liquidity provisions to local banks).

The impact on bank lending through indirect channels is also expected to be limited as long as the global financial turbulence does not widen or deepen. Bank lending could be adversely affected if mark-to-market losses originating from adverse price movements in the local equity, bond, and foreign exchange markets erode profitability and net worth. However, as local markets have generally stabilized, with limited or no net losses in asset prices so far, the impact on profitability and net worth of banks is likely to be small.

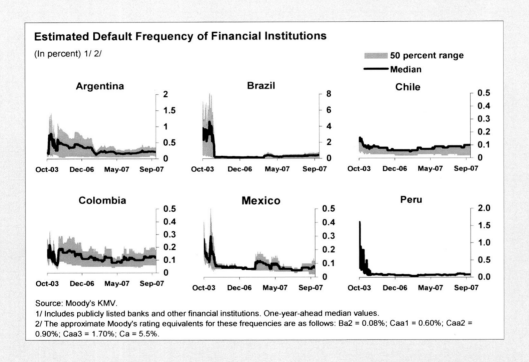

Estimated Default Frequency of Financial Institutions

(In percent) 1/ 2/

Source: Moody's KMV.
1/ Includes publicly listed banks and other financial institutions. One-year-ahead median values.
2/ The approximate Moody's rating equivalents for these frequencies are as follows: Ba2 = 0.08%; Caa1 = 0.60%; Caa2 = 0.90%; Caa3 = 1.70%; Ca = 5.5%.

Note: This box was prepared by Jingqing Chai.

Box 9 *(concluded)*

Second, the credit crunch, reflected in the higher credit default swap (CDS) spreads, and subprime losses experienced by banks in industrial countries could indirectly affect some Latin American countries, where international banks have played a role in funding local offices' domestic operations. However, recent credit growth appears to be mainly funded by local deposit growth (Chapter 2), and Latin American banking systems' foreign liabilities generally account for a small and declining part of their balance sheets. Finally, a persistent deterioration in broad credit conditions would likely have a more pronounced effect on smaller financial institutions, which are more reliant on wholesale funding from the local capital markets. This risk is mitigated by the ample capacity of most central banks to provide liquidity support in the current context of high reserves and generally stronger private and public balance sheets.

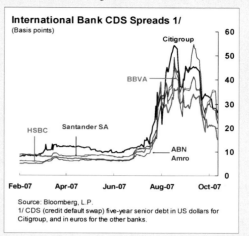

International Bank CDS Spreads 1/
(Basis points)

Source: Bloomberg, L.P.
1/ CDS (credit default swap) five-year senior debt in US dollars for Citigroup, and in euros for the other banks.

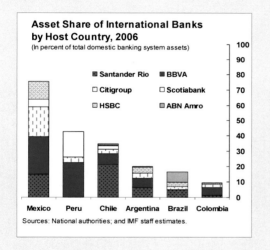

Asset Share of International Banks by Host Country, 2006
(In percent of total domestic banking system assets)

Sources: National authorities; and IMF staff estimates.

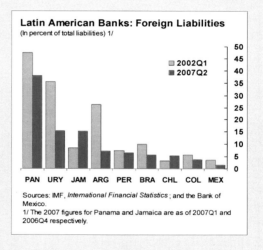

Latin American Banks: Foreign Liabilities
(In percent of total liabilities) 1/

Sources: IMF, *International Financial Statistics*; and the Bank of Mexico.
1/ The 2007 figures for Panama and Jamaica are as of 2007Q1 and 2006Q4 respectively.

---

external shocks. While larger and better-rated companies may be able to absorb the impact of shocks more easily, smaller and lower-rated companies could still be vulnerable to funding difficulties if credit conditions tighten. More broadly, continued corporate health will depend on macroeconomic stability to keep down spreads related to country and inflation risk.

In the past, domestic vulnerabilities have often amplified crises not only by exacerbating capital outflows but also by hampering the ability of domestic policy to buffer external shocks. High debt and deficits and binding public borrowing constraints often led to procyclical fiscal policy. Lack of monetary policy credibility and "fear of floating"—usually a consequence of currency mismatches in balance sheets—meant that monetary policy was also typically tightened when the external environment weakened. Today, in

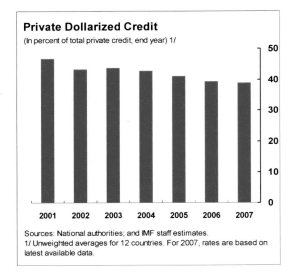

Private Dollarized Credit
(In percent of total private credit, end year) 1/

Sources: National authorities; and IMF staff estimates.
1/ Unweighted averages for 12 countries. For 2007, rates are based on latest available data.

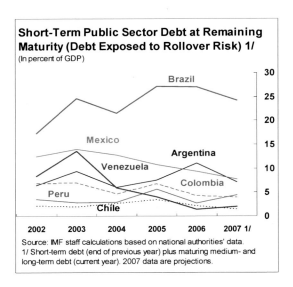

Short-Term Public Sector Debt at Remaining Maturity (Debt Exposed to Rollover Risk) 1/
(In percent of GDP)

Source: IMF staff calculations based on national authorities' data.
1/ Short-term debt (end of previous year) plus maturing medium- and long-term debt (current year). 2007 data are projections.

contrast, the prospect for effective domestic policies—particularly, monetary policy—has improved with a shift to more flexible exchange rates and relatively well-contained inflation. With currency mismatches less of a concern, several central banks allowed exchange rates to depreciate in response to the rise in risk premiums after August 2007. And with better anchored inflation expectations, the concern that exchange rate depreciations might be passed through to domestic prices does not appear to have influenced monetary policy decisions following the August turbulence.

It is sometimes argued that the favorable external environment for Latin America in the last few years—particularly high commodity prices and strong U.S. and global growth—is mainly responsible for improved fundamentals, and so these could unravel once external conditions deteriorate. While growth in Latin America is indeed sensitive to the external environment, this line of argument is too simplistic. First, Latin America has benefited from strong policies and genuine institutional improvements in recent years as well as favorable external conditions. For example, monetary policy frameworks are more credible and sophisticated, structural fiscal balances have improved even in countries that are not major commodity exporters (see Chapter 4), and many countries have implemented financial sector reforms (see Chapter 5). Second, even if

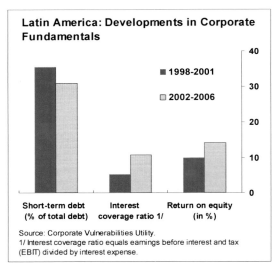

Latin America: Developments in Corporate Fundamentals

■ 1998-2001
□ 2002-2006

Short-term debt (% of total debt) | Interest coverage ratio 1/ | Return on equity (in %)

Source: Corporate Vulnerabilities Utility.
1/ Interest coverage ratio equals earnings before interest and tax (EBIT) divided by interest expense.

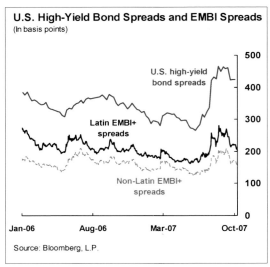

U.S. High-Yield Bond Spreads and EMBI Spreads
(In basis points)

Source: Bloomberg, L.P.

Latin America's improved economic performance were purely a result of good luck, the resulting lower public debt, higher net foreign assets, and better composition of public and private balance sheets have put the region in a better position to withstand foreign shocks than in the past. External investors so far appear to agree with this view, as evidenced in the modest increase in sovereign spreads in most Latin American countries, particularly compared with the much sharper rise in high-yield corporate bond spreads in the United States since August.[5]

This said, significant risks remain. First, fundamentals vary significantly across the region. Currency mismatch problems associated with dollar liabilities continue in some countries and, as described in Chapter 2, fast-rising government expenditures are shrinking fiscal surpluses, weakening current accounts, and contributing to inflationary pressures in several countries. Furthermore, the external crisis may widen or deepen. One risk arises from the possibility that the crisis may engulf a major emerging market country, leading to a larger reassessment of risks for the emerging market asset class than has been the case so far. Another arises from the possibility of a recession in the United States, which could significantly slow economic growth in other regions, lead to a further increase in risk premiums worldwide and weaken commodity prices. The next section employs econometric tools to study the likely effects of the August turbulence both under a relatively benign baseline for growth outside the region, and under more adverse conditions.

Scenario Analysis

This section is based on an econometric framework developed in Österholm and

Zettelmeyer (2007) for analyzing the relationship between external factors and growth in Latin America, estimated using data from 1994 until the second quarter of 2007.[6] The model focuses on six variables: an export-weighted index of world growth outside Latin America, in which the United States has a current weight of about 0.55; the U.S. short-term interest rate; the U.S. high-yield bond index as a proxy for conditions in U.S. and global credit markets; an index of net-export-weighted commodity prices relevant to Latin America; an index of aggregate growth in six large Latin American countries (Argentina, Brazil, Chile, Colombia, Mexico, and Peru); and the JPMorgan Latin America Emerging Market Bond Index (Latin EMBI). The model can generate both "unconditional forecasts," in which all these variables are forecast after conditioning only on past data, and "conditional forecasts," in which the future paths of some variables are taken as given and forecasts are derived for the remaining variables in the model. This provides an intuitive and convenient way to study Latin American growth under alternative scenarios.[7]

The baseline scenario is based on the projections for world growth and financial variables presented in the October 2007 *World Economic Outlook*. The WEO provides quarterly forecast paths for four of the six variables in the model: world growth, Latin American growth, U.S. short-term interest rates, and commodity prices. Since the objective here is to forecast Latin American growth, the WEO

---

[5] Traditionally, the EMBI and Latin EMBI spreads have reacted about one-for-one to shocks to the U.S. high-yield bond corporate spread (González Rozada and Levy Yeyati, 2006; Österholm and Zettelmeyer, 2007).

[6] See also related work by Izquierdo, Romero, and Talvi (forthcoming).

[7] Technically, the model consists of a "Bayesian Vector-Autoregression." (See Österholm and Zettelmeyer, 2007, and April 2007 *Regional Economic Outlook* for details.) The only difference between the models discussed there and the model employed in this section is that this version (1) was re-estimated on a sample including the first two quarters of 2007, and (2) uses an export-weighted index of world GDP, to better capture the impact of expected divergences between U.S. growth and economic activity elsewhere in the world. (The model discussed in the April 2007 *Regional Economic Outlook* used the IMF's GDP in PPP terms as an index of world growth).

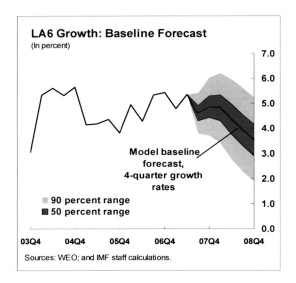

LA6 Growth: Baseline Forecast
(In percent)

Model baseline forecast, 4-quarter growth rates
■ 90 percent range
■ 50 percent range

Sources: WEO; and IMF staff calculations.

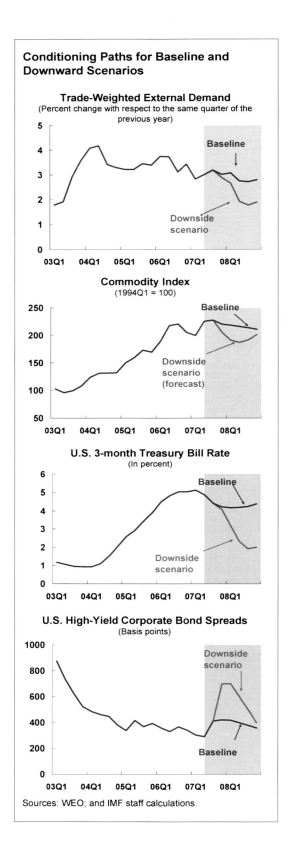

Conditioning Paths for Baseline and Downward Scenarios

Trade-Weighted External Demand
(Percent change with respect to the same quarter of the previous year)

Baseline

Downside scenario

Commodity Index
(1994Q1 = 100)

Baseline

Downside scenario (forecast)

U.S. 3-month Treasury Bill Rate
(In percent)

Baseline

Downside scenario

U.S. High-Yield Corporate Bond Spreads
(Basis points)

Downside scenario

Baseline

Sources: WEO; and IMF staff calculations.

forecast of this variable is ignored. WEO forecasts for world growth (transformed into an export-weighted index), short-term interest rates, and commodity prices are used as "conditioning paths." For the high-yield corporate bond spread, a gradual decline is assumed, albeit to levels above those preceding the August turbulence. For the Latin EMBI, no assumption is made except that the third-quarter value in 2007 (the first quarter within the forecasting period) is set equal to its actual value in that quarter. Hence, the baseline forecast of Latin American growth is conditioned on (1) the actual "shock" to credit markets observed in the third quarter of 2007; and (2) paths for world output, commodity prices, and U.S. interest rates, corresponding to the WEO's baseline forecast. As discussed in Chapter 1, the latter envisages fairly robust world growth in 2008, and only minor declines in commodity prices.

The model predicts that in this baseline scenario, Latin American growth would slow only modestly in 2008, to 4.3 percent, from 5.0 percent in 2007. The model was estimated over a sample period that includes the Latin American crises of the 1990s and, as such, has a tendency to show large reactions of growth to deteriorations of the external environment—and in particular to higher financial costs. Nonetheless, the baseline forecast broadly bears out the relatively optimistic view of regional growth laid out in the preceding section's analysis of potential transmission channels for external shocks.[8] However, the main reason is that the external baseline on which this forecast is conditioned itself remains relatively favorable. It embodies a slowdown in U.S. growth but without a recession. Moreover, the U.S. slowdown is assumed to be broadly offset by growth in the rest of the world, so that export-weighted external growth for Latin America continues essentially unchanged over the forecast period, not far below average external growth during 2004–06. Commodity prices are assumed to remain relatively high, in line with WEO projections, and corporate credit markets to return gradually to tranquil conditions, albeit with some permanent repricing of risk. Finally, the initial jump of the EMBI in the third quarter of 2007 on which the forecast is conditioned is small relative to the increases seen in previous crisis episodes. Through this channel, the simulation captures some of the improvements in Latin American fundamentals that are too recent to be reflected in the structure of the model itself.

The question remains how Latin America would react if external conditions were to deteriorate more than envisaged in the WEO baseline. An alternative scenario was constructed around the assumption that the United States suffers a recession, with negative growth in the first and second quarters of 2008, followed by a slow recovery.[9] Given the high weight of the United States in the world growth index weighted by Latin America's exports, this translates into a significant slowing of external demand growth, from 3 percent in 2007 (on an export-weighted basis) to 2.1 in 2008, about 1 percentage point

below baseline.[10] In line with the assumption that the United States slides into recession, a significant further increase of corporate spreads is assumed, to about 700 basis points, together with a reduction in U.S. short-term interest rates, as the Federal Reserve reacts to the recession. No assumptions for commodity prices or the Latin EMBI are made, that is, the model is allowed to predict these variables along with aggregate Latin American growth.

The main result is that a scenario of this type would hit Latin American growth very significantly, although it would fall short of causing a full-blown recession across the region. Specifically, the model forecasts year-on-year quarterly growth falling from 5¼ percent in the second quarter of 2007 (the last observed value) to about 4.5 percent in late 2007, then, much more steeply, to a low of 1.8 percent in the third quarter of 2008. This implies annual average growth of about 2½ percent in 2008, around 1.8 percentage points below baseline. In addition to the assumed 1 percentage point fall in external growth, this is due to the sharp tightening of external credit markets—leading to a forecast rise in the Latin

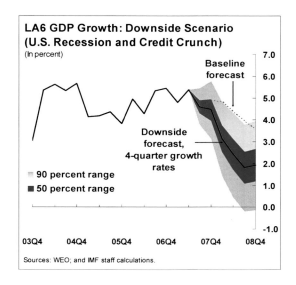

LA6 GDP Growth: Downside Scenario (U.S. Recession and Credit Crunch)
(In percent)

Sources: WEO; and IMF staff calculations.

---

[8] The model-based baseline forecast is almost identical to the forecast for Latin American growth shown in Chapter 2, which was generated independently, built up from country-level forecasts by IMF country teams.

[9] On an average annual basis, the United States is assumed to grow by 0.8 percent in this scenario, compared with projected annual growth of 1.9 in the baseline scenario.

[10] This reduction also reflects some assumed slowing of the world economy outside the United States in the event of a U.S. recession, in line with the model of Bayoumi and

(continued)

EMBI to around 600 basis points in late 2007 and early 2008—as well as a steep decline in commodity prices in this scenario. According to the model, commodity prices would fall—reflecting lower global growth—by almost 20 percent between late 2007 and mid-2008, before beginning to recover.[11]

Conclusions

A period of institutional reforms and stronger policy frameworks has left the LAC region better prepared for times of global turbulence. More flexible exchange rates have become the first line of defense against abrupt changes in capital flows, while a greater commitment to low inflation—including with the adoption of inflation-target frameworks by many countries in the region—has brought predictability and transparency to policies. Fiscal policies have also improved, leading to primary fiscal surpluses and lower debt-to-GDP ratios in the region. At the same time, governments have been able to shift their financing strategy away from bonds linked to short-term interest rates and the exchange rate toward fixed-rate and inflation-indexed paper, thus reducing the sensitivity of the public debt to temporary changes in financial conditions.

Nevertheless, important policy challenges remain, particularly if the external environment deteriorates significantly. Downside risks to U.S. growth have increased recently, raising the likelihood of a larger external demand shock to Latin America. A significant tightening in corporate credit, spurred for example by more market turbulence, could spill over to local markets in the region and cut short the ongoing credit expansion, hurting investment and growth. With improved public and private sector balance sheets and more credible policies, many of the large economies in the region are now in a position—in some cases, for the first time in decades—to respond to such a shock through countercyclical monetary policy. Indeed, a few countries may have created sufficient fiscal space to respond with countercyclical fiscal policy, should this become necessary, or at least to maintain essential spending rather than implement cuts as in earlier crises.

Even under the baseline scenario, countries face significant challenges. As discussed in more detail in the next chapter, fiscal authorities will need to reduce the pace of current expenditure growth to prevent structural fiscal surpluses from quickly turning into deficits. Monetary authorities should remain vigilant, as a mild reduction in growth in 2008 may not offset inflationary pressures from food-price increases and supply constraints. Although uncertainty about the future path of inflation has increased, improved monetary policy frameworks in many countries in the region should help them to rise to this challenge.

Swiston (2007), and consistent with the risks to world growth analyzed in the October 2007 WEO.

[11] Note that this sharp fall and incipient recovery is not an assumption but rather a model forecast conditioned on the assumed paths of world growth and financial variables.

IV. Revenue Growth and the Strength of Underlying Fiscal Positions

Fiscal balances in many Latin American countries improved steadily between 2002 and 2006. Initially, this reflected a reduction in expenditures as a share of GDP, which reached a low around 2004. Although spending picked up again in 2005 and 2006, fiscal balances continued to improve, reflecting an even greater increase in revenue growth. However, revenue ratios now appear to have stabilized, while spending growth continues unabated in many countries in the region. As a result, average fiscal balances are projected to weaken this year for the first time since 2002, with a further deterioration expected next year.

In light of continued relatively high debt levels, the region's history of fiscal weakness, and the implications of weak fiscal positions for macroeconomic volatility, a return to primary deficits in Latin America would be a cause for significant concern. Whether or not this prospect is likely to materialize in the next few years depends on two considerations:

- First, are current expenditure trends set to continue? If spending growth continues at the average rate of 8–10 percent (in real terms) experienced in the last two years, the region will probably return to primary fiscal deficits within 2–3 years, even if revenues remain at their current buoyant levels. To make room for higher capital expenditure and stabilize fiscal balances, growth of current expenditures will need to be curtailed and better targeted, particularly to social spending focused on poverty reduction.

- Second, are relatively high revenues here to stay? Answering this question requires a careful analysis of whether recent changes in revenue ratios mostly reflect "structural" shifts such as changes in tax policy, tax administration, and commodity price changes that are likely to be permanent, or temporary

Fiscal Developments, 2002-07 (In percent of GDP) 1/						
	2002	2003	2004	2005	2006	2007
Commodity Producers 2/						
Public sector revenue	24.4	25.5	26.7	28.6	30.9	30.1
Commodity revenue	4.5	6.0	6.5	8.1	9.8	9.0
Noncommodity revenue	19.9	19.4	20.2	20.5	21.0	21.0
Public sector expenditures	28.7	27.1	26.9	27.4	28.5	29.4
Current	23.5	22.0	21.5	21.3	21.6	21.7
Interest	4.8	3.6	3.2	2.6	2.5	2.5
Capital	5.2	5.2	5.4	6.0	6.9	7.8
Public sector overall balance	-4.3	-1.7	-0.1	1.2	2.4	0.6
Public sector primary balance	0.5	2.0	3.1	3.9	4.9	3.1
Noncommodity Producers 2/						
Public sector revenue	24.2	24.5	24.4	25.2	26.2	26.3
Public sector expenditures	28.2	28.2	27.0	26.9	27.1	27.7
Current	23.6	23.4	22.4	22.3	22.7	22.8
Interest	3.8	3.8	3.4	3.2	3.0	2.8
Capital	4.7	4.8	4.6	4.6	4.4	4.9
Public sector overall balance	-4.0	-3.7	-2.6	-1.7	-0.9	-1.4
Public sector primary balance	-0.3	0.2	0.8	1.5	2.2	1.4

Source: IMF staff estimates.
1/ Unweighted averages.
2/ Commodity producers: Argentina, Bolivia, Chile, Colombia, Ecuador, Mexico, Peru, Trinidad and Tobago, and Venezuela. Noncommodity producers: Brazil, Costa Rica, Guatemala, Honduras, Nicaragua, Panama, Paraguay, El Salvador, and Uruguay.

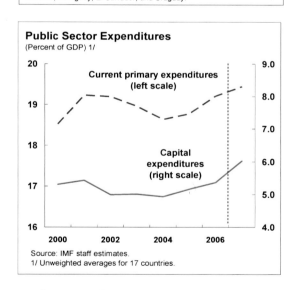

Public Sector Expenditures
(Percent of GDP) 1/

Source: IMF staff estimates.
1/ Unweighted averages for 17 countries.

factors such as cyclical tax buoyancy, or commodity price increases that may be reversed over the medium term.

The remainder of this chapter provides such an analysis of structural revenues and fiscal balances.[12] Reflecting the special role of commodity-related revenues in the recent increase in revenue ratios in many Latin America countries, commodity revenues and noncommodity revenues are analyzed separately. To assess the medium-term prospects for commodity revenues, current revenues are adjusted in line with expected movements in relevant commodity prices. Noncommodity revenues are analyzed using econometric techniques, decomposing the observed revenue ratio into the level that would be expected, given the current state of the tax system, if the economy were in a "neutral" cyclical position; the portion that is attributable to the business cycle; and a residual, which could reflect other factors bearing on the tax ratio—such as changes in tax compliance or relative price movements—that may or may not be temporary. Finally, the results from these two steps are combined with data on noninterest expenditures to generate an overall view of the "structural" primary fiscal balance, that is, the primary balance if output were at a cyclically neutral position, commodity prices were at their medium-term expected prices, and both the tax system and expenditures were to remain unchanged. The structural primary balance hence gives a sense of the "underlying" strength of the fiscal position, abstracting from cyclical or temporary factors.

The main results are as follows. First, for most countries analyzed, structural primary balances are currently weaker than actual (i.e., reported) primary balances. Hence, focusing on actual balances in Latin America somewhat exaggerates the strength of the underlying fiscal position. This is particularly true for nonfuel commodity exporters, since nonfuel commodity prices are projected to decline significantly in the medium term. Second, in most countries in which the primary balance is currently reported to be in surplus, the structural primary balance is also likely to be in surplus, albeit at a lower level. Since these

are presently the majority of countries in the region, this is also true on average. Third, structural balance calculations in some countries are subject to a large margin of uncertainty, either because of uncertain commodity price projections, or because a significant portion of recent changes in noncommodity revenues as a share of GDP cannot be easily attributed *either* to cyclical conditions or to changes in the tax system. The assessment of the fiscal position in these countries hence depends on how this "residual" change in the revenue ratio is interpreted. Finally, the prospects for maintaining a structural primary surplus going forward will first and foremost depend on countries' success in curbing the pace of spending growth. If spending were to continue to grow at its current pace, it is possible that the region's structural surplus might disappear as early as next year.

Structural Commodity Revenues

Unlike tax revenues related to economic activity, such as income or consumption, commodity-related revenues depend on commodity prices and production volumes.[13] The latter are usually viewed as "structural," in the sense that they are determined by natural resource endowments and policy decisions. Hence, estimating structural commodity revenues is a matter of adjusting actual commodity revenues for medium-term expected changes in commodity prices. As a result, the estimation of structural commodity revenues is sensitive to the commodity price forecasts that enter in the adjustment.

To obtain an idea of this sensitivity, the analysis in this chapter uses two sources for price forecasts: IMF projections of commodity prices, which are

---

[12] See also related work by Izquierdo, Ottonello, and Talvi (forthcoming).

[13] "Commodity revenues" are defined as fiscal revenues that can be attributed to the activities of commodity-producing industries, whether from income and profit taxes, VAT, royalties, or export taxes. In the analysis that follows, commodity revenues are only analyzed for countries in which they exceed 2 percent of GDP.

primarily based on futures prices, and are available over a five-year period; and projections from the World Bank, which are based on an econometric model, and are available for a somewhat longer period, until 2015. Using data from these two sources, commodity price indices were constructed for nine major commodity producers in the LAC region—defined as countries with at least 2 percent of GDP commodity revenue.[14] "Structural commodity revenue" was then defined as actual revenue divided by the ratio between current and five-year expected average commodity prices, for each country, according to either IMF or World Bank projections.

As is clear from the charts, the commodity price projections have a significant impact on the results. IMF projections for commodity prices suggest that structural commodity revenues have been rising in line with actual commodity revenues in most of the countries analyzed. (This is less true for Chile—as copper prices are projected to decline substantially over the medium term—and also for Peru and Bolivia, where commodity price declines are also expected to reduce revenue somewhat). In contrast, the World Bank projects lower medium-term prices for most commodities exported from Latin American countries, including energy. This translates into a generally more pessimistic view of underlying structural commodity revenues.

The difference across the two sets of projections matters particularly for oil producers. IMF projections, based on futures markets, forecast continued high oil prices in the medium term. But the model-based projections by the World Bank envisage a significant decline in oil prices (on the order of 25 percent) over the next five years, and an even bigger drop by 2015. As a result, structural commodity revenues estimated using these price projections are currently below actual commodity revenues by 3–4 percent of GDP in

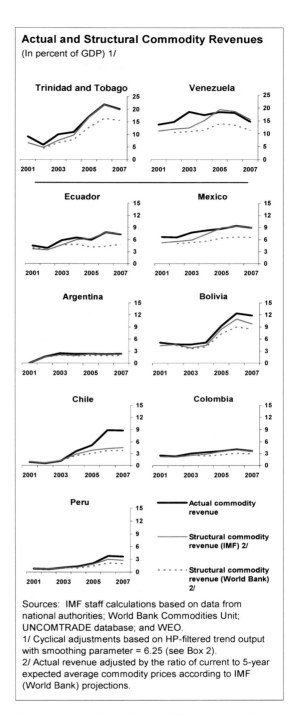

Actual and Structural Commodity Revenues
(In percent of GDP) 1/

Sources: IMF staff calculations based on data from national authorities; World Bank Commodities Unit; UNCOMTRADE database; and WEO.
1/ Cyclical adjustments based on HP-filtered trend output with smoothing parameter = 6.25 (see Box 2).
2/ Actual revenue adjusted by the ratio of current to 5-year expected average commodity prices according to IMF (World Bank) projections.

[14] Namely, Argentina, Bolivia, Chile, Colombia, Ecuador, Mexico, Peru, Trinidad and Tobago, and Venezuela.

Venezuela and Trinidad and Tobago, and by around 2 percent in Ecuador and Mexico. In contrast, estimates based on the IMF price projections imply that current revenue levels will be sustained over the medium term, provided that production volumes are maintained.

Structural Noncommodity Revenues

The standard approach to estimating "structural" noncommodity revenues (see, for example, Hagemann, 1999) is to apply a cyclical adjustment to the reported revenue ratios. The extent of this cyclical adjustment will depend on two factors (see Appendix for details): the cyclical position—that is, whether the economy is deemed to be far away from a neutral cyclical state or not, see Box 2—and the "income elasticity of revenue," which measures how much revenues tend to respond to changes in economic activity. If the income elasticity of revenue is 1—that is, revenues respond proportionally to changes in output—then the economic cycle has no impact on the revenue-to-GDP ratio, and the reported ratio will be deemed entirely "structural." Similarly, if the income elasticity of revenue is different from 1 but actual output is close to potential output, then any cyclical adjustment to the reported revenue ratio will also be very small.

As it turns out, for the eight countries whose revenues are analyzed in this section[15] the cyclical adjustment is very small for one or the other of these reasons. For three countries, estimated income elasticities were very close to 1 (a standard result). For four others, Costa Rica, Colombia, El Salvador, and Peru, the estimated elasticity was between 1.1 and 1.2; and for Panama it was 0.8 (see Appendix). However, the "output gaps" (deviations from neutral cyclical positions) for these countries are currently estimated to be small. As a result, any cyclical adjustment to revenue/GDP ratios is very minor. This methodology would therefore suggest that current noncommodity revenue ratios in these countries should be viewed as almost entirely "structural," and hence permanent.

However, this conclusion is subject to an important caveat. In the standard cyclical adjustment approach, any change in revenue ratio that is not identifiably cyclical is assumed to be "structural," whether or not it can be accounted for by changes in the tax system. This constitutes a potentially significant weakness in the methodology, as some of the supposedly noncyclical changes in revenue may well be due to one-off factors, which could be reversed in the future. The standard analysis was therefore extended by an additional step, which sought to quantify the impact of identifiable changes in the tax system on revenue, on the basis of either an econometric approach or direct estimates from country authorities or IMF staff (see Appendix).

In three of the eight countries analyzed here, identifiable changes in the tax system together with identifiable cyclical effects explain almost all of the recent changes in revenue ratios. But in the remaining countries, unexplained residuals are significant—about 1 percentage point of GDP or more. Argentina and Panama, in particular, show large positive residuals in 2006 and 2007—that is, reported revenue is higher than can be explained by identifiable cyclical or identifiable structural factors—while for Chile one finds a large negative residual. These residual revenues could be viewed as transitory, reflecting one-off increases or decreases in revenue that are likely to disappear, at

Changes in Noncommodity Revenue, 2002-06 (In percent of GDP) 1/					
	Total	Identifiably cyclical 3/	Identifiably structural 4/	Residual	
Argentina 2/	2.87	0.00	0.42	2.46	
Brazil	0.28	0.00	0.68	-0.40	
Chile	-2.58	0.00	0.04	-2.63	5/
Colombia	2.67	0.02	1.40	1.25	
Costa Rica	1.12	0.05	1.10	-0.03	
El Salvador	2.24	0.00	2.18	0.06	
Panama	1.72	-0.03	-0.39	2.14	
Peru	0.02	0.02	0.95	-0.96	

Source: National authorities, and IMF staff calculations.
1/Refers to central government revenue.
2/ 2003-2006, as 2002 was a crisis year.
3/ Based on estimation; see appendix.
4/ Owing to changes in the tax system and tax progressivity.
5/ Reflects increases in the GDP deflator driven by copper prices (see text).

---

[15] Argentina, Brazil, Colombia, Costa Rica, Chile, El Salvador, Panama, and Peru. The sample was limited because the analysis requires extensive information on changes in the tax system and their revenue impact, which is available only for some countries.

least over the medium term. But they could also reflect unaccounted but nonetheless permanent structural changes, for example, unaccounted improvements in tax administration.

Information about the specific source of revenue strength or weakness can sometimes provide clues. In the case of Chile, for example, an unexplained reduction in the ratio of noncommodity revenue to GDP appears to be driven not by lower revenues but by an increase in the GDP deflator, as copper price increases have outpaced the increase in consumer prices that drive VAT collection. For Argentina, the unexplained portion of the surge in revenues could be a result of improvements in tax administration or of faster economic growth in sectors with a higher tax burden. Improvements in tax administration could also play a role in explaining the surge in Panama.

Statistical criteria can also help decide whether unaccounted surges should be viewed as transitory. Intuitively, a rise in residual revenues is more likely to reflect a structural shift if it is large relative to past fluctuations in the revenue-to-GDP ratio, and if it has already been sustained for several years. Formal statistical tests suggest that for most countries analyzed, residual changes in revenue tend to disappear over time (they appear to be "stationary"; see Appendix for details). For the most part, therefore, it is wise to treat residual revenue buoyancy as temporary rather than structural. One significant exception is Argentina, for which statistical tests cannot reject that residuals persist over time.

To summarize, while standard cyclical adjustment suggests that current high levels of noncommodity revenues in many countries are largely structural, not all of these increases can be accounted for by changes in the tax system. Based on their statistical properties, these unaccounted "residuals" should generally be regarded as temporary. One exception is Argentina, which experienced a large shift in revenue several years ago—with little tendency to revert over time—

which at this point is most plausibly regarded as structural.

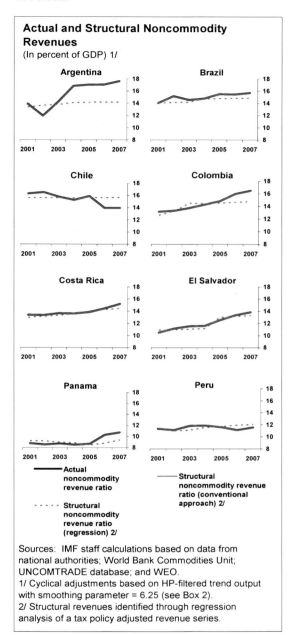

Actual and Structural Noncommodity Revenues
(In percent of GDP) 1/

Sources: IMF staff calculations based on data from national authorities; World Bank Commodities Unit; UNCOMTRADE database; and WEO.
1/ Cyclical adjustments based on HP-filtered trend output with smoothing parameter = 6.25 (see Box 2).
2/ Structural revenues identified through regression analysis of a tax policy adjusted revenue series.

Expenditures

Unlike in industrial countries, expenditure commitments tied to the economic cycle (for example, unemployment benefits) do not play a major role in Latin American budgets. For this reason, the standard approach in the fiscal literature on Latin America is to assume that all government expenditure in these countries is "structural," i.e., driven by policy, without an automatic countercyclical link to output and employment. In fact, expenditures in Latin America have in the past tended to be procyclical (Clements, Faircloth, and Verhoeven, 2007). Governments took advantage of buoyant revenue to expand expenditure in good times, and were forced to compress it in bad times owing to weak fiscal positions, and resultant borrowing constraints or high borrowing costs. Looking forward, we examine how strong underlying fiscal positions in the region would be now on the assumption that primary expenditures are independent of the cycle.

Even if expenditures are assumed to be noncyclical, computing the expenditure to GDP *ratio* when the economy is in its cyclically neutral position—in analogy to the structural revenue ratios shown in the figures of the previous sections—requires an adjustment to the observed expenditure to GDP ratio.[16] However, for most countries in the region the gap between actual GDP and potential GDP has not been large in recent years. Consequently, spending ratios expressed as a share of potential output closely track reported spending ratios. Both concepts show a sharp rise in spending ratios in many countries in the region, particularly among the energy exporters, and the larger economies. Exceptions include Chile, Panama, and El Salvador.

Structural Primary Balances

Using the structural revenue estimates and noninterest expenditure data, it is possible to derive a set of tentative estimates of structural primary balances. These give a sense of the overall strength of the fiscal position in the countries analyzed. Two additional assumptions need to be

---

[16] When actual GDP is above trend (or "potential") GDP, the reported spending-to-GDP ratio is reduced, as the denominator is larger than it would be at potential, and vice versa.

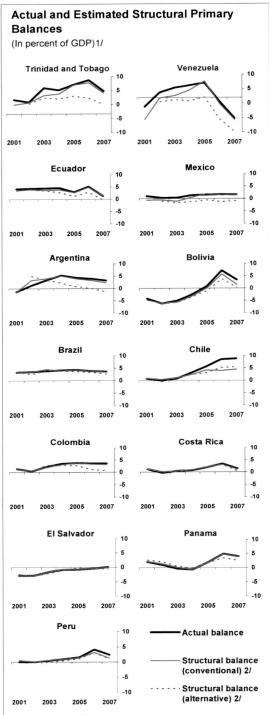

Actual and Estimated Structural Primary Balances
(In percent of GDP)1/

Sources: IMF staff calculations based on data from national authorities; World Bank Commodities Unit; UNCOMTRADE database; and WEO.
1/ Cyclical adjustments based on HP-filtered trend output with smoothing parameter = 6.25 (see Box 2).
2/ "Conventional" estimates view all noncyclical revenues as structural and use IMF commodity price projections; "alternative" excludes regression residual from definition of noncommodity structural revenues and uses World Bank projections.

made to overcome data difficulties. First, for commodity producers whose noncommodity structural revenues could not be analyzed in detail, the standard methodology for calculating cyclically adjusted revenues is applied using the average revenue elasticity estimated for the other countries in the region (about 1.1). Second, since commodity revenues often accrue to public enterprises, we focus here on overall *public sector* structural balances. This requires taking a view on structural, or permanent, noncommodity revenues outside the central government. For this purpose, we assume that all noncyclical changes in such revenues are structural.

The evolution of alternative structural balance estimates since 2002 allows some general conclusions:

- With few exceptions, 2006 and projected 2007 structural primary balances remain in positive territory, although with large margins of uncertainty. In some cases, uncertain and conflicting commodity price projections, particularly for oil, cloud the picture.[17] In others, including Argentina, Panama, and Colombia, there is uncertainty on how much of the large recent increases in noncommodity revenue should be viewed as permanent—although this uncertainty can in some cases be narrowed by examining the statistical properties of the estimated residuals, as discussed earlier.

- However, a significant deterioration of both actual and structural fiscal balances is expected for this year, driven by sharply rising expenditure ratios.

---

[17] The calculations for Chile are broadly consistent with the government's structural surplus target when similar commodity price projections are used (note that the government's surplus target refers to the overall structural balance of the central government whereas the results here refer to the structural *primary* balance for the overall *public sector*).

Conclusions

Many Latin American countries made impressive improvements in fiscal positions between 2002 and 2006. This has been a crucial factor in reducing vulnerability to external shocks, as evidenced by the region's relative resilience so far following the recent financial market turbulence. Following an initial period earlier in this decade of expenditure restraint, these fiscal improvements have recently come from the revenue side. These improvements have in part been driven by tax policy and administrative changes but also by rising commodity revenues, and in some cases by increases in noncommodity revenues that are difficult to explain either by cyclical conditions or explicit policy and administrative improvements. Statistical analysis suggests that—for the most part—these residual increases in revenue should be viewed as temporary.

Underlying structural primary balances still generally appear to be in surplus in the countries in which reported balances are in surplus. However, these surpluses are more modest than the unadjusted data indicate, particularly in commodity-exporting countries facing possible declines in prices over the medium term.

Actual and Structural Primary Balances, Public Sector (In percent of GDP)						
	2006				2007	
	Actual	Structural 1/		Pro- jected	Structural 1/	
		Max	Min		Max	Min
Argentina	4.0	3.7	0.0	3.3	2.8	2.1
Bolivia	7.2	5.8	3.6	3.4	1.5	0.2
Brazil	3.9	4.1	3.1	3.6	3.8	2.5
Chile	8.5	5.7	3.2	8.8	6.3	3.7
Colombia	3.4	3.1	1.1	3.6	3.4	0.7
Costa Rica	3.4	3.2	2.8	1.4	1.2	0.3
Ecuador	5.1	4.9	2.8	1.3	1.4	-0.4
El Salvador	-0.4	-0.3	-0.7	0.1	0.3	-0.4
Mexico	1.7	1.5	-1.3	1.6	1.6	-0.9
Panama	4.9	4.8	3.4	3.9	3.9	2.5
Peru	4.1	4.2	2.2	2.4	2.2	0.5
Trinidad & Tobago	8.8	7.9	2.3	4.8	4.1	-0.3
Venezuela	0.6	0.0	-5.6	-5.2	-3.7	-9.9

1/ Estimates. "Max" uses most favorable commodity price forecasts and assumes that any positive (negative) revenue "residuals" are *permanent* (transitory). "Min" uses least favorable commodity price forecasts and assumes that any positive (negative) revenue "residuals" are *transitory* (permanent) except for Argentina, where Min estimates assume that the (positive) residuals are permanent, based on the statistical properties of the residuals (see text and appendix table). If the residuals for Argentina are assumed to be transitory, the "Min" estimate for Argentina would be reduced to -1.4 from 2.1.

Furthermore, primary surpluses will significantly shrink this year, as expenditure ratios continue to rise while revenue ratios stabilize. If expenditure growth is not curtailed, fiscal balances will quickly erode, and the region could soon return to primary deficits.

In some countries, better control of expenditures may require institutional or structural reforms. International experience suggests that expenditure rules can be helpful but need to be supported by broad political consensus, consistent revenue policy, and in some cases expenditure reforms. Depending on country circumstances, such reforms could include reducing budgetary rigidities (Alier, forthcoming), increasing expenditure efficiency and flexibility, and strengthening public financial management systems.

Appendix. Estimation of Structural Revenue and Structural Balances

Methodology

Commodity Structural Revenue

Commodity revenues depend on commodity production or export volumes, prices, and the fiscal regime. Fiscal regimes and production/export volumes are taken to be part of the "structure" that in principle is under the control of the authorities. Hence, making the same functional form assumption as is commonly made in the literature on noncommodity structural revenue (see below), $R_t^c = \beta p_t^\gamma$, and $R_{s,t}^c = \beta p_t^{*\gamma}$, where p_t^* is the long-run commodity price expected at time t, R_t^c stands for commodity revenues, β and γ are parameters, and the subscript s is used to denote structural revenue. Substituting β, it follows that

$$(1) \qquad R_{s,t}^c \equiv R_t^c \left(\frac{p_t^*}{p_t} \right)^\gamma .$$

In the absence of reliable country-specific estimates for γ, this study follows the Chilean approach (Marcel and others, 2001) and assumes that $\gamma = 1$ for all countries. p_t^* is based on five-year-ahead commodity price forecasts published separately by the IMF (in the *World Economic Outlook*) and the World Bank—i.e., $p_t^* = E[p_{t+5}]_t$. In either case, export-share-weighted commodity price indices were created for each country, so that p_t^* is a weighted average of the expected prices of each commodity exported by that country.

Note that the above relationships do not explicitly recognize the role of the exchange rate in translating dollar commodity revenues into local currency revenues (implicitly, the exchange rate is subsumed in the parameter β). This is admissible so long as the exchange rate is close to its equilibrium value, which is an acceptable assumption for most countries studied here. If exchange rates are not close to equilibrium, this would create an additional reason why structural commodity revenues could be different from actual revenues. An undervalued exchange rate implies that structural commodity revenues are lower than actual revenues, while an overvalued currency implies that they are higher.

Noncommodity Structural Revenue

The standard approach to estimating noncommodity structural revenue (see, in particular, Hagemann, 1999; see also Chalk, 2002) starts by assuming a constant elasticity relationship between revenue, R, and its tax base (for example, GDP or national income, denoted Y):

$$(2) \qquad R_t^{nc} = A Y_t^\varepsilon .$$

Using a star to denote potential output, it follows that $R_{s,t}^{nc} = A Y_t^{*\varepsilon}$. Substituting the parameter A, structural revenue can hence be estimated by applying a simple cyclical correction to actual revenue:

(3) $\hat{R}_{s,t}^{nc} \equiv R_t^{nc}\left(\dfrac{Y_t^*}{Y_t}\right)^{\hat{\varepsilon}}$,

where the $\hat{\varepsilon}$ is either an estimate of the revenue elasticity using time-series data for R_t and Y_t or an assumed value (most studies indicate that $\hat{\varepsilon}$ is in a narrow range between about 1 and 1.25).

A potential problem with this approach arises from the fact that, for any specific $\hat{\varepsilon}$ and A, $R_t^{nc} \neq AY_t^{\hat{\varepsilon}}$; that is, $R_t^{nc}/Y_t^{\hat{\varepsilon}} \equiv A_t$ is not constant over time. However, it could still be the case that $R_{s,t}^{nc} = AY_t^{*\varepsilon}$, i.e., that the parameters A and ε define the (unobservable) relationship between structural balances and potential output. In that case, computing structural balances as

$$R_{s,t} \equiv R_t^{nc}\left(\dfrac{Y_t^*}{Y_t}\right)^{\hat{\varepsilon}}$$

amounts to assuming that $A = A_t$ —that is, that the "structural" parameter A shifts in every period in line with the actual realization of revenues in relation to GDP. In other words, in the standard approach, *any change in revenues that cannot be explained by cyclical factors is considered structural.*

This is implausible in many cases, as fluctuations in A_t may reflect one-off or other factors that are reversed over time, consistent with a long-run stable A. Indeed, it could be the case that there are no structural breaks in A other than these associated with identifiable policy actions, which can be accounted for using dummy variables or by adjusting the data. This hypothesis can be tested by testing for the existence of a long-run "co-integrating" relationship between the (adjusted) R_t^{nc} series and Y_t , that is, testing the proposition that although R_t^{nc} and Y_t are "integrated"—i.e., follow a stochastic trend—the residual from a regression of one on the other is stationary. If this can be confirmed, it implies that *any change of (tax-policy-adjusted) revenues that cannot be explained by cyclical factors should be considered temporary.*

Structural revenues would then be given by the fitted values in the regression of R_t^{nc} on Y_t , evaluated at a cyclically neutral level,

(4) $\tilde{R}_{s,t}^{nc} = \hat{A}Y_t^{*\hat{\varepsilon}}$,

plus any effect of tax policy changes that was previously removed from the series in order to estimate the parameters in the above equation.

This study uses both approaches, that is, Equations (3) and (4), to derive alternative estimates of the noncommodity structural revenues, based on the output gap estimates presented in Box 2, and the parameter estimates discussed below (see Vladkova-Hollar and Zettelmeyer, 2007). Underlying the figures in Chapter 2 is a set of potential output/output gaps based on the Hodrick-Prescott filter with the "smoothing parameter" λ set at 6.25. Output gaps according to the other concepts discussed in Box 2 were used for robustness checks. Final results are expressed as a share of GDP (see below).

Structural Balances

By definition, the structural balance equals structural revenue minus structural expenditures:

(5) $B_{s,t} \equiv R_{s,t} - E_{s,t} \equiv R_{s,t}^{nc} + R_{s,t}^{c} - E_{s,t}$,

where B stands for balance and E for expenditure (or noninterest expenditure, if the focus is the structural *primary* balance), and the remaining notation is unchanged. In line with the literature on Latin America (see, for example, Alberola Ila and Montero, 2006), it is assumed that all expenditure is structural: $E_{s,t} = E_t$. Structural revenues are computed as described in the previous two subsections.

The structural balance as a share of GDP is obtained by dividing both sides by potential output $Y_t^* \equiv Y_t/g$, where g denotes the output gap (expressed as a ratio). Using lower-case letters to denote shares of current GDP and setting $\gamma = 1$, this yields, based on Equation (3):

(6) $$\frac{\hat{B}_{s,t}}{Y_t^*} = r_t^{nc} g_t^{1-\hat{\varepsilon}} + r_t^c \frac{E[p_{t+5}]_t}{p_t} g_t - e_t g_t$$

and based on Equation (4):

(7) $$\frac{\tilde{B}_{s,t}}{Y_t^*} = A Y_t^{*(\hat{\varepsilon}-1)} + r_t^c \frac{E[p_{t+5}]_t}{p_t} g_t - e_t g_t \, .$$

Estimation

Estimation of noncommodity structural revenues according to Equation (4) involved the following steps.

For countries considered commodity producers (which, in this context we define as having commodity-related revenues in excess of 2 percent of GDP), the central government revenue series was adjusted to exclude commodity revenues. For each country, the resulting noncommodity-related central government revenue series was then adjusted for the impact of changes in tax policy. The preferred methodology was to directly adjust the revenue series for the effect of changes in the tax structure through available impact estimates (IMF staff reports, working papers, country tax authorities' estimates, authors' own estimations). In cases in which a direct estimate could not be obtained, the effect of changes in the tax structure was controlled for through step dummies. Particular effort was made to avoid dummies in the latter part of the sample (2004–06), where a dummy would likely pick up some of cyclical improvement along with the effect of tax policy. This could not be avoided in the case of Costa Rica, where the introduction of automation in customs administration was launched in 2005.

The ordinary-least-squares estimates of the long-run policy-adjusted income elasticity of

Long-Run Income Elasticity of Central Government Tax Revenues
(OLS estimates, standard errors in parentheses)

| | Estimated income elasticity | Evidence for Cointegration | | | |
| | | (Number of CI vectors) | | ADF test (test statistic) 1/ | KPSS test (test statistic) 2/ |
		Trace test	Max. Eigenvalue		
Argentina	0.99 (0.01)	1	0	-2.36	0.26**
Brazil	1.03 (0.01)	1	1	-1.96	0.18*
Chile	1.01 (0.03)	0	0	-2.42	0.14
Colombia	1.09 (0.05)	1	1	-2.11	0.21**
Costa Rica	1.11 (0.02)	1	1	-4.92***	0.17
El Salvador	1.16 (0.25)	1	1	-2.609	0.09*
Panama	0.80 (0.16)	0	0	-1.95	0.11
Peru	1.15 (0.07)	1	1	-3.67	0.23***

1/ *, **, and *** denote rejection of the null hypothesis that the residuals are nonstationary at the 10%, 5%, and 1% significance level, respectively. Critical values for the Dickey-Fuller *t*-statistics when applied to residuals are taken from Hamilton (1994), Table B.9.
2/ *, **, and *** denote rejection of the null hypothesis that the residuals are stationary at the 10%, 5%, and 1% significance level, respectively. Critical values for the KPSS LM-statistics when applied to residuals are taken from Shin (1994), Table 1.

noncommodity central government tax revenues suggest that the estimated income elasticity is significantly different from unity only in Brazil and Costa Rica. In Panama, the lower point estimate of the income elasticity of tax revenues could perhaps be explained by the lack of full inclusion of the some dynamic sectors of the economy in the tax base. In most countries there is evidence of co-integration according to both the Johansen and the Engle-Granger tests. The main exceptions are Argentina, Chile, and Panama. However, for Chile and Panama the null hypothesis that the residuals in the relationship between GDP and revenue are stationary could not be rejected, whereas it could be rejected at the 5 percent level in the case of Argentina.

V. Financial Sector Development in Latin America: Recovery or Overheating?

In Latin America and the Caribbean, local credit and capital market activity have picked up strongly in recent years, with bank credit growing in double digits in several countries (see Chapter 2). As the external environment becomes more challenging, the question arises to what extent this increased intermediation mirrors the region's rising resilience and not a renewed buildup in vulnerabilities.

This chapter examines the characteristics of recent financial sector developments in the LAC region to shed light on the sustainability of the region's recent rapid credit and financial sector growth, focusing particularly on bank credit. The analysis addresses three questions. The first is whether rapid increases in bank credit and capital market activity have been associated with deepening and broadening of markets, as measured by underlying improvements in banking efficiency, market liquidity, and the number of new stock or bond issues. The second is whether the strong credit growth observed in several countries signals an excessive credit boom that cannot be sustained, or is more likely to reflect mostly improved macroeconomic and institutional fundamentals. The third issue concerns the key regulatory and institutional challenges remaining in the region, based on a survey of recent financial sector assessments.

Financial Deepening or Bubbles

Financial deepening strengthens an economy's resilience to adverse shocks through stronger financial institutions, greater risk diversification, and more efficient allocation of capital, which also promotes economic growth. Stock and bond market development contributes to growth through the creation of liquidity, which makes investment less risky and more attractive while companies raise long-term capital (Levine, 1996).

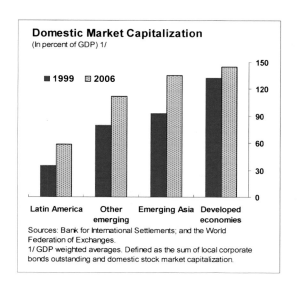

Domestic Market Capitalization
(In percent of GDP) 1/

■ 1999   ▦ 2006

Sources: Bank for International Settlements; and the World Federation of Exchanges.
1/ GDP weighted averages. Defined as the sum of local corporate bonds outstanding and domestic stock market capitalization.

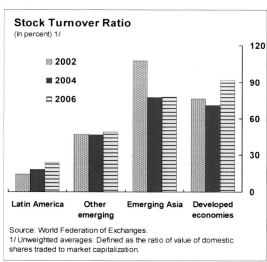

Stock Turnover Ratio
(In percent) 1/

▦ 2002
■ 2004
▤ 2006

Source: World Federation of Exchanges.
1/ Unweighted averages. Defined as the ratio of value of domestic shares traded to market capitalization.

Well-functioning derivatives markets can contribute to this process through risk sharing and lowering the costs of managing complex risks.

Latin America's financial markets continue to lag those in other emerging markets. Recent data show that this remains the case, as measured by bank credit–to-GDP ratios, market capitalization, and capital raised in equity markets. Market liquidity for both stocks and corporate bonds also remains relatively low in the region.

However, recent developments in the region indicate some genuine deepening and broadening in the LAC region's financial markets. First, overhead costs, a measure of banking intermediation efficiency, have declined since 2001. Second, domestic stock and corporate bond markets in the larger Latin American countries have expanded in terms of total capitalization, although partly driven by higher asset prices (see Chapter 2). Third, markets have become more liquid on various measures, including the total values of stocks and bonds traded measured relative to market capitalization (i.e., turnover ratio), as a share of GDP, and relative to market volatility. Fourth, new stock and corporate bond listings across the region, although still low, have risen. They reached an annual average of 8 and 200, respectively, during the period 2004–06, compared with 4 and 155 during the previous three-year period. Finally, markets for exchange-traded foreign exchange derivatives and over-the-counter foreign exchange and interest rate derivatives have expanded in several countries (see Box 10).

Credit Boom or Recovery

Recent rapid growth in bank credit needs to be viewed in light of the preceding long period of declining credit-to-GDP ratios (see the November 2006 *Regional Economic Outlook*). Moreover, to the extent that economic growth brings with it a certain degree of financial deepening, bank credit should be expected to follow a rising trend during an economic expansion such as the region has been experiencing. But as double-digit credit growth has continued in a number of countries across the region, it is important to evaluate whether this growth is sustainable. This is especially true for Latin America given the region's history of susceptibility to "boom-bust" credit cycles.

In this section, two approaches were used to identify a potentially unsustainable credit boom: deviations of bank credit–to-GDP ratio from trend levels (Gourinchas, Valdés, and

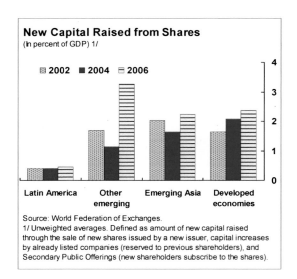

New Capital Raised from Shares
(In percent of GDP) 1/

Source: World Federation of Exchanges.
1/ Unweighted averages. Defined as amount of new capital raised through the sale of new shares issued by a new issuer, capital increases by already listed companies (reserved to previous shareholders), and Secondary Public Offerings (new shareholders subscribe to the shares).

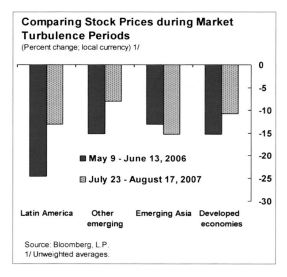

Comparing Stock Prices during Market Turbulence Periods
(Percent change; local currency) 1/

Source: Bloomberg, L.P.
1/ Unweighted averages.

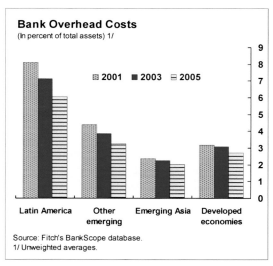

Bank Overhead Costs
(In percent of total assets) 1/

Source: Fitch's BankScope database.
1/ Unweighted averages.

Box 10. Derivatives Markets in Latin America

Well-functioning derivatives markets can provide significant benefits to corporations, financial institutions, and institutional investors by allowing them to improve risk management and lower funding costs. For example, greater accessibility and diversity of derivatives help alleviate exchange rate risk facing Latin American firms and facilitate commodity price hedging in some of the region's largest economies.

Partly reflecting these benefits, derivatives trading has surged in the larger economies in the region. Brazil, Mexico, Colombia, and Chile combined registered a daily trading volume of close to US$110 billion (notional) in 2006. Interest rate derivatives (swaps, options, and forward rate agreements) represented about 70 percent of total trading activity. Currency derivatives (FX forwards and swaps) have been growing rapidly in the wake of increased exchange rate and capital account flexibility as well as greater trade and financial integration. The use of other derivatives, such as those on local credit, remains limited.

With an average daily trading volume of US$46 billion in 2006, Brazil boasts the largest derivatives market in Latin America, followed closely by Mexico and Argentina. Trading activity in Brazil is dominated by exchange-traded interest rate and currency futures, while over-the-counter (OTC) derivatives trading (mainly interest rates) is relatively minor. In contrast, derivatives trading in Mexico and Argentina is focused on currency-based instruments (mostly on very short-term government debt) and commodities respectively.

In other countries in the region, derivatives trading is much smaller and occurs mostly OTC in either FX or fixed income assets. In Chile, trading is concentrated in onshore, short-term, OTC-traded FX derivatives contracts and in offshore nondeliverable forwards, motivated by limited foreign holdings in the domestic bond market, high transaction costs onshore, and regulatory limits on pension funds' use of interest rate swaps and forwards. The derivatives market in Colombia is considerably smaller.

There is scope to develop these markets further, while strengthening regulatory oversight to mitigate potential downside risks. Reform priorities could include:

- *Strengthening the regulatory and legal frameworks for derivatives markets.* Best practices include consistent capital rules, collateral requirements, and netting provisions; transparency-enhancing full balance sheet disclosure; accounting rules aligned with international accounting standards; a tax environment that creates a level playing field for all cash and derivatives trading; and provisions for short-selling.

- *Fostering exchange-based derivatives trading.* In Mexico, MexDer offers a diverse set of derivatives instruments, and a well-functioning electronic settlement and clearing system enhances effective monitoring of trading activity and efficient execution of trades. In Brazil, BM&F has a solid track record in product innovation, asset diversification, and broadening of investor base. Both Colombia and Costa Rica are exploring possibilities to expand existing and create new exchanges for derivatives trading.

- *Encouraging a broad and balanced investor base for genuine hedging.* For derivatives markets to be effective, especially in dollarized countries, the creation of complementary hedging interest is critical. Commercial banks with short-term liabilities (and long-term fixed-rate holdings) and institutional investors with long-term, foreign currency holdings have complementary term structures, with the latter acting as net suppliers of foreign currency or floating rate sellers. Removing limits or prohibitions on pension funds and insurance companies thus helps promote hedging and capital market liquidity in general. For example, the recent elimination of investment limits and transaction taxes for foreign investors in Mexico helped increase local bond market liquidity.

Note: This box was prepared by Andreas Jobst.

Landerretche, 2001) and a comparison of actual bank credit–to-GDP ratio with the estimated "potential" level, given a country's macroeconomic and institutional fundamentals.

In the first approach, the underlying trend is measured using a country-specific filter. A credit boom is identified when the deviation of the actual credit-to-GDP ratio from this estimated trend exceeds a given threshold. Threshold values are defined in terms of both absolute deviation (i.e., the simple difference between actual and trend credit to GDP) and relative deviation (i.e., the difference between actual and trend credit to GDP in percent of trend credit to GDP). The threshold values are selected so that they capture most of the past episodes of credit booms and/or banking crises (see Appendix).

In recent years, all but 6 of the 20 largest countries in Latin America and the Caribbean experienced increases in credit to the private sector relative to GDP. In 12 of these, sharp increases in credit pushed the ratio of credit to GDP over its trend level (see panel chart on actual and trend private sector credit). However, until 2006, no country experienced credit growth in excess of the "threshold" values for defining a boom. Last year, continued credit expansion pushed credit above one or both thresholds in five countries: Colombia, Honduras, Jamaica, Mexico, and Nicaragua. Past credit booms typically lasted several years before collapsing, although they suggest that continued debt expansion at this pace could warrant concern. It is thus too soon to conclude that these developments constitute an excessive or unsustainable "boom."

Credit booms may also be identified on the basis of predictions of an economic model that links credit to fundamentals. The capacity for a country's banking system to extend credit safely to the private sector depends both on economic conditions and on the quality of financial and public institutions. In this context, a credit "boom" could be viewed as credit growth that cannot be justified by economic fundamentals and institutional factors.

How do LAC countries measure up against other regions in the key determinants of financial development identified in the literature? As a number of authors have pointed out (de la Torre Gozzi, and Schmukler, 2006; and Braun and Hausmann, 2003), the still relatively low level of financial development is disappointing, given that several countries in the region have undertaken significant financial sector reform efforts since the 1980s. A regional comparison of underlying institutional determinants of financial development shows that while the LAC region is relatively strong in areas such as credit information and credit bureaus, it remains weak in areas such as creditor rights and governance. Moreover, even with the recent macroeconomic improvements, inflation and real interest rates also remain relatively high.

How empirically important are these weaknesses in holding back financial development in the Latin American and the Caribbean region? New econometric analysis using a panel of 79 countries over the period of 2001–05 shows that inflation, institutional quality (as measured by the World Bank's governance index), and real deposit interest rates have significant effects on the ratios of private sector credit to GDP. For example, a 1 percentage point improvement in each of these dimensions is associated with an increase in private sector credit of over 1 percent of GDP.

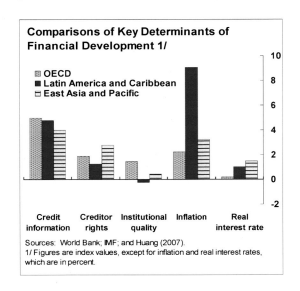

Comparisons of Key Determinants of Financial Development 1/

OECD
Latin America and Caribbean
East Asia and Pacific

Credit information · Creditor rights · Institutional quality · Inflation · Real interest rate

Sources: World Bank; IMF; and Huang (2007).
1/ Figures are index values, except for inflation and real interest rates, which are in percent.

The effectiveness of creditor rights protection, captured by the variable "legal origin," is also shown to matter—legal reforms toward stronger protection of creditors and investors may be expected to lead to significant increases in private sector credit relative to GDP.[18] Finally, productivity growth that leads to higher GDP per capita may also help boost credit intermediation. Given these results, where then do LAC countries stand relative to their "potential"?

A comparison of actual credit to GDP with the level that would be predicted by the model shows that many of the 20 largest LAC countries have been performing below their model-fitted potentials in recent years (see panel chart on actual and fitted credit). Of the five largest emerging markets in LAC, only Brazil has bank lending to the private sector at a level close to its "potential," whereas Chile, Mexico, Peru, and Colombia have still to benefit from their relatively strong fundamentals. Under this criterion, there is no indication of excess credit growth in Colombia and Mexico. Four countries—Bolivia, Haiti, Honduras, and Panama—are found to have credit-to-GDP ratios higher than their model fitted potentials. However, in two of these cases—Bolivia and Panama—higher-than-predicted credit ratios reflect the slow unwinding of credit booms during the 1990s rather than recent credit expansion. In the case of Haiti, it reflects the collapse (and slow recovery) of fundamentals as a result of political and social strife.

Slow adjustment of actual credit to improvements in fundamentals—either as a result of reforms in the 1990s and this decade, or from postcrisis recoveries—could also be the reason why bank credit remains below "potential" in many Latin American countries. In addition, credit levels that appear to trail fundamentals could reflect factors that are not included in the analyses but nevertheless tend to reduce credit intermediation,

such as financial transaction taxes, interest rate controls, and directed lending.

In summary, the two commonly used criteria for "excess" credit growth analyzed for the region suggest that much of the recent credit growth seems to be generally associated with improvements in fundamentals, and that there are not yet clear signs of general overheating in the region. This finding is consistent with the latest prudential indicators and equity market–based bank solvency estimates, which show that nonperforming loan ratios and banks' estimated default probabilities have remained at low levels (see Chapter 2 and Box 9). However, the aggregate picture may mask heightened vulnerabilities in certain financial institutions that have lowered credit standards in their pursuit of rapid expansion. While the extent of such vulnerabilities is not clear owing to the difficulty in obtaining up-to-date information on the institutional distribution of credit growth, the rapid pace of credit growth in some countries warrants enhanced regulatory oversight and prompts measures to strengthen supervisory capacity.

Regulatory Responses and Options

A survey based on Financial Sector Assessment Programs (FSAPs) and IMF Article IV consultations for the region shows that, while considerable progress has been made in strengthening and developing the region's financial sectors, there remains scope for improvement in a number of areas. First, enhancing regulatory independence and risk-based supervisory capacity remains a top priority in many countries, especially where credit has been growing rapidly. Second, significant increases in foreign participation in several local capital and credit markets make effective consolidated and cross-border supervision more important. Third, the increasing role of nonbank financial institutions such as finance houses and mutual funds present a new regulatory challenge. Fourth, improving bank resolution framework and

---

[18] Following La Porta and others (1998), common-law countries generally protect investors the most, and civil-law countries protect them the least.

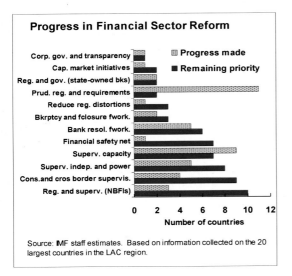

Progress in Financial Sector Reform

Corp. gov. and transparency
Cap. market initiatives
Reg. and gov. (state-owned bks)
Prud. reg. and requirements
Reduce reg. distortions
Bkrptcy and fclosure fwork.
Bank resol. fwork.
Financial safety net
Superv. capacity
Superv. indep. and power
Cons.and cros border supervis.
Reg. and superv. (NBFIs)

☒ Progress made
■ Remaining priority

0 2 4 6 8 10 12
Number of countries

Source: IMF staff estimates. Based on information collected on the 20 largest countries in the LAC region.

financial safety nets (such as the clarification of lender-of-last-resort functions and the role of deposit insurance, and crisis contingency planning) will be important to sustained financial stability. Finally, the recent growth in the derivatives markets in several Latin American countries makes it important for regulators to be able to monitor and evaluate the risks associated with financial innovations. The experience of the relatively developed markets in the region (mainly Brazil, but also Chile and Mexico) points to the importance of regulatory measures, disclosure requirements, and documentation standards for compliance with capital rules and smooth functioning of the derivatives markets.

Conclusions

Underpinned by institutional reforms and stronger policy frameworks, the region's financial markets have deepened and broadened over the past several years. The analysis in this chapter suggests that recent rapid credit growth observed in the region mostly represents a continued catching up in the level of financial intermediation, following earlier crises and important financial sector reforms. However, the pace of credit growth indicates that heightened regulatory oversight may be needed in coming years. As governments in the region recognize, further reforms to deepen and broaden financial markets, and strengthen the

institutional structure, will be important to bolster resilience going forward.

Appendix. Estimation Methods, Variable Definitions, and Data Sources

Two types of analyses are conducted in this chapter to give a range of indications for the extent that credit growth has exceeded a given trend level.

Filter-Based Trend Analysis

We derived the trend by applying a retrospective rolling Hodrick-Prescott filter for each country. This approach can be economically meaningful in that the threshold is selected based on past episodes of credit booms and/or banking crises. Threshold values are defined in both relative deviation (i.e., the difference between actual and trend credit-to-GDP ratios relative to trend credit-to-GDP ratio) and absolute deviation (i.e., the difference between actual and trend credit-to-GDP ratio). The former adjusts for the different degree of financial deepening, and the latter for the different size of economy. A relative threshold of 18 percent and/or an absolute threshold of 3 percent capture a majority of the past credit booms or banking crises (e.g., 1994–97 Mexico crisis, 1994–99 Brazil crisis, 1981–83 Chile crisis, and 2002–03 Uruguay crisis).

The IMF's *International Financial Statistics* data on banks' claim on private sector and nominal GDP are used for the period of 1960–2006, and *World Economic Outlook* projections for nominal GDP are used for 2007 so that bank credit–to–GDP ratios are calculated as bank credit of the current year divided by the average of the current year GDP and the following year GDP.

Estimation of the "Potential" Level of Bank Credit to GDP

We included both economic fundamentals and policy and institutional variables that are found

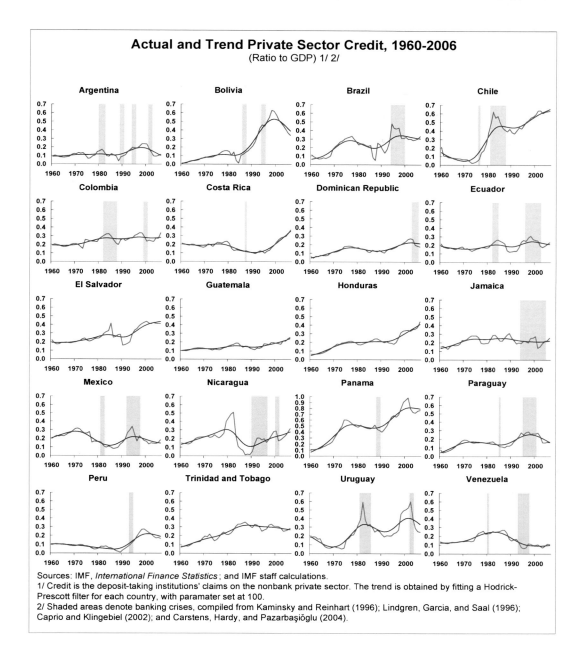

Actual and Trend Private Sector Credit, 1960-2006
(Ratio to GDP) 1/ 2/

Sources: IMF, *International Finance Statistics*; and IMF staff calculations.
1/ Credit is the deposit-taking institutions' claims on the nonbank private sector. The trend is obtained by fitting a Hodrick-Prescott filter for each country, with paramater set at 100.
2/ Shaded areas denote banking crises, compiled from Kaminsky and Reinhart (1996); Lindgren, Garcia, and Saal (1996); Caprio and Klingebiel (2002); and Carstens, Hardy, and Pazarbaşiöğlu (2004).

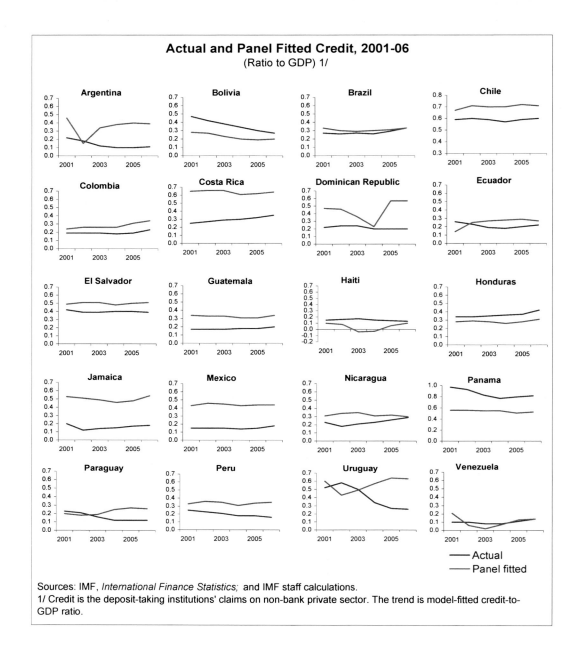

Actual and Panel Fitted Credit, 2001-06

(Ratio to GDP) 1/

Sources: IMF, *International Finance Statistics;* and IMF staff calculations.

1/ Credit is the deposit-taking institutions' claims on non-bank private sector. The trend is model-fitted credit-to-GDP ratio.

important for financial development in the literature. Djankov, McLiesh, and Schleifer (2006) found that both creditor protection through the legal system and information sharing institutions are associated with higher ratios of private credit to GDP, although the former is relatively more important in the richer countries and the latter in developing countries. A study by Huang (2007) found that trade openness and governance have positive effects on financial development, whereas civil legal origin, inflation volatility, and policy instability have negative effects on financial development. He also found initial conditions and geography important—countries with a smaller land area, higher initial GDP and population, more open trade policy, and stronger institutions have a higher level of financial development. A recent study by Dehesa, Druck, and Plekhanov (2007) found that higher credit-to-GDP ratios are associated with stronger creditor rights and lower inflation.

We used GMM IV regressions to formally estimate the effects of various factors on the banks' credit to private sector as percent of GDP. Because of the possible endogeneity from using the concurrent level of GDP per capita, it was instrumented using lagged values of explanatory variables, as well as initial GDP and population and an index of ethnic fractionalization. The first-stage regression results suggest that endogeneity is indeed a problem, and IV relevance test and overidentification test support the use of these instruments. Time dummies are included to capture changes over time in global markets and domestic banking structure.

The table on p. 63 shows results from the preferred regression specifications, which are generally robust to changes in specifications. The estimates are similar to those found in the

literature, with coefficients generally having the expected signs.[19]

The estimations of the "potential" level of bank credit to GDP are based on a panel of 79 countries from 2001 to 2005. Annual data for PPP-adjusted real GDP per capita, which are measured in 2000 international dollars, and CPI indices are taken from the World Bank's World Development Indicators database. Data for bank credit to the private sector relative to GDP are from the World Bank's new database on financial development and structure. Data for deposit interest rates are taken from the IMF's International Financial Statistics database; where deposit interest rates are not available, treasury bill rates are used. Data for trade restrictiveness are taken from the IMF's trade policy information database, which includes ratings based on tariff structures and nontariff trade barriers. The ratings take the value of 1 to 10, with 10 being the most restrictive in trade regime.

The main data for institutional quality are from the World Bank and Huang (2007). Governance and institutional quality is the simple average of the six measures of institutional development: voice and accountability, political stability, government effectiveness, regulatory quality, rule of law, and control of corruption, based on extensive surveys conducted by Kaufmann, Kraay, and Mastruzzi (2007). Credit information and private and public credit bureau coverage (as percent of total adult population) are taken from the World Bank's Doing Business database. Indexes of shareholder rights and creditor rights are based on La Porta and others (1998) and range from 0 to 6 and 0 to 4, respectively, with higher values being stronger rights.

---

[19] Contrary to Huang (2007), trade restrictiveness is associated with higher credit-to-GDP ratio. While this may reflect the lack of variation in data, one possible explanation is that countries that are less open are also protective of their domestic banking sector, promoting domestic financing of trade.

The instrumental variables (real GDP per capita and total population in 1990, and index of ethnic fractionalization) are taken from the Penn World Tables 6.1 and Alesina and others (2003), respectively. The legal origin dummy for the French, German, and Scandinavian systems is based on the World Bank's Global Development Network database. Data for the land area in square kilometers is based on Gallup, Sachs, and Mellinger (1999).[20]

Summary of "Credit Boom" Episodes, 1980-2006			
	Relative Threshold = 18%	Absolute Threshold=3%	Banking Crisis 1/
Argentina	1980-82, 1998-2000	1980-81, 1998-2000	1980-82, 1989-90, 1994-95, 2001-02
Brazil	1988, 1994-97	1988, 1994-97	1990, 1994-99
Chile	1981-84	1980-85, 2001-02	1981-87
Colombia	1984, **2006**	1982-84, 1996-98, **2006**	1982-87, 1999-2000
Mexico	1992-94, **2006**	1992-94, **2006**	1982, 1992-97
Peru	1981-85, 1997-99	1997-2000	1993-94
Honduras		1987-88, 1998-99, 2006	
Boliva	1982, 1999	1982, 1993-94, 1997-2000	1986-87, 1994-95
Uruguay	1981-82, 1998-2002	1981-83, 1998-2002	1981-84, 2002-03
Costa Rica			1987
Dominican Republic	2000-01	2001-03	2003-05
Ecuador	1983-86, 1997-98	1983-86, 1995, 1997-98	1982-84, 1996-2002
El Salvador	1985	1983-85, 1989, 1997-2000	
Guatemala	1983-84	1983-84	
Jamaica	1989, 1998-99	1982-83, 1988-89, 1998-2000, **2006**	1994-2000
Nicaragua	1980-82, 1992-93, 1999-2000	1980-82, 1992-93, 1998-2000, **2006**	1990-96, 2000-01
Panama	2001	1987, 1994, 1998-2000	
Paraguay	1982, 1994	1994, 1997, 2001	1985, 1995-2000
Trinidad and Tobago		1985, 1987, 1998	
Venezuela	1987, 1997, 2005	1986-87	1993-95

1/ Crisis episodes as identified by Caprio and Klingebiel (2002); Carstens, Hardy, and Pazarbasioglu (2004); and Kaminsky and Reinhart (1996).

[20] Data for most of the time invariant variables are obtained from Huang (2007).

62

GMM IV Regression Results
(Dependent variable: private sector credit to GDP) 1/

	Coefficients	P-Value	Coefficients	P-Value	Coefficients	P-Value
Log of real GDP per capita, PPP adjusted	0.11	0.00	0.10	0.00	0.11	0.00
Land area in log	-0.04	0.00	-0.03	0.00	-0.03	0.00
Credit information index	0.01	0.31	0.01	0.21	0.01	0.21
Inflation	-0.71	0.00	-0.72	0.00	-0.69	0.00
Real interest rates	-0.27	0.12	-0.27	0.11	-0.28	0.10
Governance and institutional quality	0.19	0.00	0.18	0.00	0.18	0.00
Civil legal origin dummy	-0.07	0.01	-0.07	0.01	-0.08	0.00
Trade restrictiveness	0.10	0.03	0.01	0.02		
International Financial Center			0.09	0.23	0.08	0.27
Constant	0.03	0.73	0.02	0.80	0.01	0.89
Number of observations	370		370		370	
Centered R-squared	0.76		0.76		0.76	
Uncentered R-squared	0.90		0.90		0.90	

1/ Instrumented: log of real GDP per capita, PPP adjusted. Excluded instruments: Index of ethnic fractionalization, log of real GDP per capita in 1990, log of population in 1990.

Summary Statistics on Key Indicators of Financial Development
(Average of 2001-05, unless noted otherwise)

	OECD		Latin America and Caribbean		East Asia and Pacific		Middle East and North Africa		Europe and Central Asia		South Asia		Sub-Saharan Africa	
	Mean	Obs.	Mean	Obs.	Mean	Obs.	Mean	Obs.	Mean	Obs.	Mean	Obs.	Mean	Obs.
Institutional quality														
Legal rights index	6.3	88	3.8	80	6.5	52	3.8	48	5.6	72	4.8	16	4.5	87
Credit information index	5.0	109	4.8	98	4.0	52	2.9	48	3.2	89	3.0	16	1.3	87
Private credit bureau coverage	8.8	88	10.9	80	4.9	52	10.0	48	2.5	72	0.2	16	1.5	87
Public credit bureau coverage	59.0	84	38.5	80	36.9	44	14.6	48	9.9	64	2.6	16	4.4	87
Shareholder rights index 1/	3.0	88	2.7	36	3.4	40	2.2	20	2.0	4	4.3	12	0.9	13
Creditor rights index 1/	1.9	88	1.3	32	2.8	40	2.5	16	2.0	4	3.7	12	1.3	13
Civil legal origin dummy	0.7	109	0.9	98	0.3	52	0.8	48	1.0	5	0.0	16	0.6	87
Governance index	1.4	109	-0.3	98	0.4	52	0.1	48	-0.2	5	-0.6	16	-0.6	87
Trade restrictiveness	3.7	109	3.4	98	2.9	52	5.2	36	4.8	5	6.1	16	3.7	87
Initial conditions														
Log 1990 population	9.8	109	9.2	98	10.0	48	9.5	36	10.9	5	11.6	16	9.2	87
Log 1990 real GDP per capita	9.8	109	8.3	98	8.9	48	8.7	36	8.7	5	7.5	16	7.1	87
Log land area	11.8	109	12.5	98	11.5	52	12.4	48	13.6	5	12.8	16	12.2	87
Ethnic fractionalizaion index 2/	0.2	104	0.4	98	0.3	52	0.3	48	0.3	5	0.4	16	0.7	87
Macroeconomic environment														
PPP-based real GDP per capita	27117.8	109	5693.0	98	13307.4	52	11188.7	48	8050.5	74	2490.8	16	1904.2	87
CPI inflation	2.2	109	9.1	98	3.3	52	3.2	48	7.3	77	5.9	16	8.0	87
Real interest rate	0.2	93	1.0	98	1.5	52	2.0	38	2.2	69	0.8	12	1.1	80

Sources: World Bank; IMF; and Huang (2007).
1/ Based on La Porta and others (1998).
2/ Based on Alesina and others (2003).

VI. Caribbean Economic Outlook and Integration Issues

Recent Developments and Economic Outlook

Caribbean growth performance has been robust and the outlook remains favorable. Last year, regional GDP expanded by 5½ percent—the fastest pace in over two decades.[21] Strengthened policy frameworks and a favorable external environment have underpinned the recovery since 2001, when tourism receipts declined sharply in the wake of the events of September 11. Looking ahead, growth is expected to slow moderately, reflecting the ending of Cricket World Cup (CWC)-related activity and a return to trend for tourism earnings after 2006, when visitors were diverted to the Caribbean from hurricane-affected Mexican destinations. With the external outlook still broadly favorable, Caribbean growth is, nonetheless, expected to remain above historical norms, with regional GDP expanding by about 4 percent in 2007 and 2008.

Strengthened macroeconomic policies have helped contain inflation. Countries in the region have generally been successful at limiting the inflationary impact of natural disaster–related food supply shocks and higher petroleum import prices. Skillful conduct of monetary policy in Jamaica has led to a reduction in consumer price inflation from 19 percent in September 2005 to under 6 percent by end-2006. Similarly, inflation in the Dominican Republic, which accelerated sharply in the wake of the banking crisis in 2002–03, was reversed once the authorities regained control over monetary aggregates. Inflation has, however, remained an issue in Trinidad and Tobago, where

---

[21] Caribbean average is the arithmetic average of the following 15 Caribbean countries: Antigua and Barbuda, The Bahamas, Barbados, Belize, Dominica, Dominican Republic, Grenada, Guyana, Haiti, Jamaica, Trinidad and Tobago, St. Kitts and Nevis, St. Lucia, St. Vincent and the Grenadines, and Suriname.

Real GDP Growth
(Annual percent change)

Source: WEO.
1/ Unweighted average.

Output Growth
(In percent; annual rate)

	1995-2004 Avg.	2005	2006	2007 Proj.	2008 Proj.
The Caribbean 1/	4.2	6.5	8.4	6.0	4.4
The Bahamas	3.3	2.5	3.4	3.1	4.0
Barbados	2.2	4.1	3.9	4.2	2.7
Dominican Republic	5.2	9.3	10.7	8.0	4.5
ECCU economies 1/	2.7	5.5	5.8	3.6	3.9
Guyana	2.4	-1.9	5.1	5.6	4.6
Haiti	1.5	0.4	2.2	3.2	4.3
Jamaica	0.5	1.4	2.5	1.4	2.0
Trinidad & Tobago	7.7	8.0	12.0	6.0	5.8

Source: WEO.
1/ PPP-weighted average.

the positive terms of trade shock and rapid growth of public investment have led to the emergence of capacity constraints. On balance, average inflation in the Caribbean is projected to accelerate slightly to 5 percent in 2007 and decline further over the medium term.

Inflation
(In percent; end of period rate) 1/

	1995-2004 Avg.	2005	2006	2007 Proj.
The Caribbean 2/	**11.0**	**8.3**	**6.1**	**6.5**
The Bahamas	1.7	1.2	2.3	2.6
Barbados	2.5	7.4	5.6	4.9
Dominican Republic	13.0	7.4	5.0	6.0
ECCU economies 2/	2.0	4.4	2.2	3.4
Guyana	5.4	8.3	4.2	8.0
Haiti	17.1	14.8	12.4	8.0
Jamaica	11.5	12.9	5.8	8.9
Trinidad & Tobago	4.2	7.2	9.1	8.0

Sources: WEO; and IMF staff estimates.

1/ End-of-period rates, i.e. December on December. These will generally differ from period average inflation rates quoted in the *World Economic Outlook*, although both are based on identical underlying projections.

2/ PPP-weighted average.

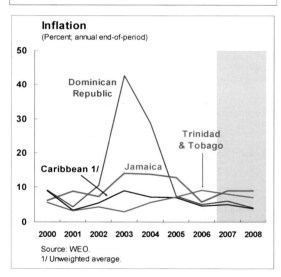

Inflation
(Percent; annual end-of-period)

Source: WEO.
1/ Unweighted average.

Countries in the region took advantage of the economic expansion early on to strengthen fiscal balances. On average, deficits improved by 4 percentage points of GDP during 2002–05 owing to a variety of policy initiatives. For example, Dominica overhauled the tax system and cut the wage bill after its economic crisis in 2002–03, while Jamaica adopted its own ambitious program of fiscal consolidation under which a range of revenue and expenditure measures were implemented during 2003–04. Several Caribbean countries also embarked on tax reforms, such as the introduction of a VAT, which has helped

strengthen revenue collections (Antigua and Barbuda, Dominica, Guyana, and St. Vincent and the Grenadines). Moreover, budgets have weathered adverse developments more successfully in recent years because of reforms to

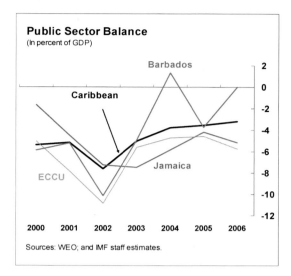

Public Sector Balance
(In percent of GDP)

Sources: WEO; and IMF staff estimates.

enhance fiscal flexibility, such as mechanisms to keep domestic petroleum prices more closely aligned with import costs. More recently, however, fiscal efforts have waned in some instances. Jamaica's primary surplus declined in 2006 and deficits widened in the countries of the Eastern Caribbean Currency Union (ECCU).

The outlook for the Caribbean will continue to depend on external events as well as domestic policy responses. The Caribbean region is highly exposed to the risk of shocks, and downside risks have increased in a number of respects. Hurricane

External Current Account
(In percent of GDP)

	1995-2004 Avg.	2005	2006	2007 Proj.	2008 Proj.
The Caribbean 1/	**-3.4**	**-0.3**	**-0.4**	**-1.0**	**-0.6**
The Bahamas	-10.1	-14.3	-25.4	-21.1	-16.5
Barbados	-4.0	-12.5	-8.4	-8.6	-8.5
Dominican Republic	-0.9	-1.4	-3.2	-3.4	-2.3
ECCU economies 1/	-15.9	-19.8	-24.9	-22.0	-20.6
Guyana	-11.9	-15.5	-17.5	-19.7	-17.0
Haiti	-1.1	1.8	0.6	2.1	1.5
Jamaica	-5.9	-11.2	-11.1	-10.9	-10.8
Trinidad & Tobago	2.2	23.8	25.6	19.7	17.2

Source: WEO.
1/ Dollar-weighted GDP average.

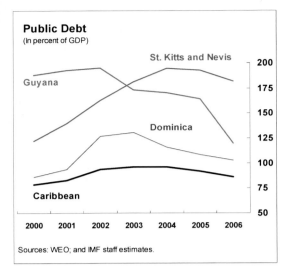

Public Debt
(In percent of GDP)

Sources: WEO; and IMF staff estimates.

fiscal targets consistent with achieving the benchmark. Similarly, Jamaica is aiming for an improved primary surplus target this year.

Regional Integration Issues

Caribbean economies have historically been among the most open in the world. While this allows the Caribbean to reap the benefits of trade integration and globalization, it also poses challenges, particularly in light of the small size of many Caribbean countries. Regional cooperation can help overcome many of these challenges. Pooling resources, for example, helps the region take advantage of scale economies and share risk. Similarly, strengthening regional collaboration enables Caribbean countries to compete more effectively for productive foreign investment and adjust to changes in global trade patterns.

Dean, which swept through the Caribbean in late August, has lowered the growth outlook and increased inflation risk in a number of affected countries (in particular Dominica, Jamaica, and St. Lucia). Moreover, ongoing volatility in international financial markets could have an adverse impact on global growth, thus weakening prospects for Caribbean tourism and growth. The Caribbean remains, in particular, very dependent on developments in North America, given the strong linkages through tourism, remittances, and foreign investment flows. Thus, any slowdown in economic activity in the United States will have an adverse impact on Caribbean growth prospects.

Further progress at reducing debt is critical to improving resiliency to shocks. Fiscal consolidation earlier during this economic cycle, in combination with debt restructuring in some cases, has led to a decline in debt ratios since 2003. Nevertheless, Caribbean countries continue to rank among the most heavily indebted countries in the world, with some posting debt-to-GDP ratios well above 100 percent. Looking ahead, the region remains committed to further debt reduction. For example, in 2006 the ECCU reconfirmed its objective of reducing public debt in all its member countries to below 60 percent of GDP. A revised benchmark for reaching the target by 2020 has been adopted, and ECCU countries have committed to establishing annual

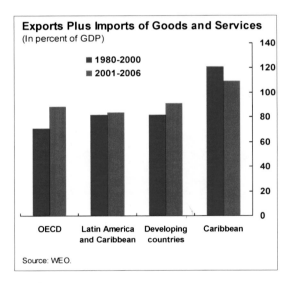

Exports Plus Imports of Goods and Services
(In percent of GDP)

■ 1980-2000
■ 2001-2006

Source: WEO.

Three areas that relate to integration are currently high priorities: first, regional financial integration, as a means of developing and deepening financial systems and ultimately raising regional growth; second, tax incentives and investment, where harmonized regional action is key to overcoming collective action problems; and third, devising strategies to manage the erosion of trade preferences in EU export markets. The remainder of this chapter summarizes key issues in these areas (see Rodlauer and others, forthcoming, for details).

Financial Integration

The Caribbean Community (CARICOM), established in 1973 and currently comprising 15 countries, is seeking to integrate national capital markets by removing restrictions on the provision of financial services and regional cross-border capital flows. Total financial sector assets in CARICOM exceed 150 percent of regional GDP, including sizable nonbanking as well as banking sectors, and the financial sector accounts for about 8 percent of regional output, above the G7 average of 7 percent. Regional financial conglomerates play a large role in the Caribbean, with combined assets of the nine largest financial conglomerates almost equivalent to regional GDP. The region's financial center is Trinidad and Tobago, where the financial sector accounts for one-tenth of that country's GDP, comparable to the share in Singapore.

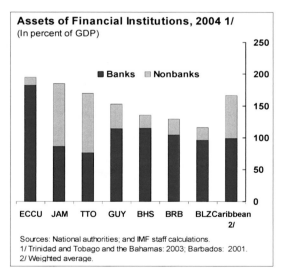

Assets of Financial Institutions, 2004 1/
(In percent of GDP)

■ Banks □ Nonbanks

ECCU   JAM   TTO   GUY   BHS   BRB   BLZ   Caribbean 2/

Sources: National authorities; and IMF staff calculations.
1/ Trinidad and Tobago and the Bahamas: 2003; Barbados: 2001.
2/ Weighted average.

While Caribbean financial markets are large in relation to GDP, they are generally not well developed. For example, regional primary bond markets are dominated by government securities, with illiquid secondary markets and outdated settlement and custody systems. Similarly, stock market turnover remains low by international

standards. Trade in financial derivatives is also limited, and takes place over the counter, given the absence of secondary markets and organized exchanges.

Notwithstanding the framework provided by CARICOM, national financial markets in the Caribbean remain fairly segmented. Cross-border banking activity is limited, and regional offshore borrowing remains relatively small. Further evidence of segmentation is provided by uncorrelated interest rates, a relatively high degree of interest rate dispersion, and large and persistent price differences for cross-listed stocks. Integration could increase the availability of capital, especially to small firms and countries; spur improvements in financial regulations and standards; reduce the cost of capital; and, in the process, raise economic growth by helping channel resources to economic activities providing greater rates of return.

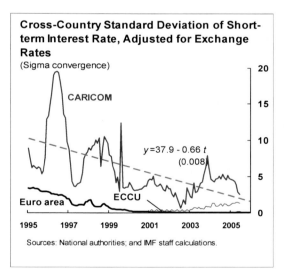

Cross-Country Standard Deviation of Short-term Interest Rate, Adjusted for Exchange Rates
(Sigma convergence)

CARICOM

$y = 37.9 - 0.66\,t$
(0.008)

Euro area   ECCU

1995   1997   1999   2001   2003   2005

Sources: National authorities; and IMF staff calculations.

Improving prospects for integration and avoiding its pitfalls requires strong policies. One side effect of integrated financial markets is that shocks can spread across borders much more rapidly. Strengthened macroeconomic policies and conditions help limit contagion, especially for countries with high debt and large external current account deficits. Intra-Caribbean capital account liberalization, a central component of financial integration, also requires greater flexibility on the part of the monetary authorities. Some countries in the region need, in particular, to ensure that their market-based monetary policy instruments are adequate to manage liquidity in an integrated environment. Finally, stronger infrastructure and simpler trading rules can reduce transaction costs and market segmentation.

Successful integration will also require strengthened regulatory oversight, particularly over regional conglomerates. Integration can introduce risks that are not yet known and, more generally, render the assessment and management of risks more difficult at the national level. As regional conglomerates increasingly become organized less along jurisdictional lines and more along functional lines, regional supervisors will, in particular, be challenged to ensure that "blind zones" do not emerge from segmented knowledge and/or jurisdictions. While Caribbean countries are taking steps to strengthen oversight, a number of issues merit greater priority in the regional context: continuing with efforts to improve supervision at the national levels; strengthening crisis management preparedness; and improving regional coordination on safety net and resolution issues for regional banks or groups.

Tax Incentives and Investment

Policymakers across the Caribbean have actively relied on incentives to attract FDI and generate jobs. As a result, there has been a proliferation of special investment incentives throughout the region, typically tax holidays that exempt corporations from income taxes and import duties for up to 25 years. With increased global capital mobility, regional governments have hesitated to reduce existing incentive schemes unilaterally, out of concern that investment will flow to other countries.

However, despite the widespread existence of incentives, the Caribbean's share of regional and global investment has stagnated. FDI has grown in the Caribbean, but no faster than elsewhere in the world. The intraregional distribution of FDI is

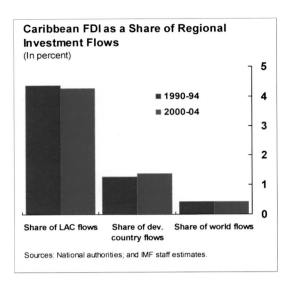

Caribbean FDI as a Share of Regional Investment Flows
(In percent)

Sources: National authorities; and IMF staff estimates.

also uneven—the largest economies received the bulk of the investment flows into the Caribbean, but the smaller ECCU countries stand out as the largest recipients of FDI when measured relative to GDP. Furthermore, FDI flows are highly persistent over time in individual countries and tend to be concentrated in key export sectors, reflecting natural endowments.

Recent work by IMF staff confirms earlier findings emphasizing the importance of factors other than incentives in attracting investment. It shows that FDI in the Caribbean is sensitive to tax policy but only to a limited extent; other factors such as institutional quality, infrastructure development, governance, openness, and FDI restrictions are at least as important. Notably, FDI incentives do not appear to have a significant effect on FDI flows in a large developing country sample, although they matter in the sample of just Caribbean countries.

Tax and tariff incentives can also be costly. These costs include (1) eroding the tax base; (2) distorting resource allocation; (3) increasing administrative burdens; and (4) creating opportunities for rent seeking. While a thorough cost analysis is precluded by data limitations, the gap between annual revenues implied by statutory rates and actual collections is upward of 10 percent of GDP a year on average for the

Potential Less Actual Taxes, 1995-2004 (In percent of GDP) 1/			
	Corporate Income Taxes	Import-related Taxes	Total
Caribbean	5.6	5.3	10.9
Dominican Republic	4.0	3.9	7.9
Trinidad and Tobago	3.3	2.4	5.7
Jamaica	6.2	3.9	10.1
ECCU	5.4	5.8	11.2
Other	6.1	5.7	11.8

Source: Rodlauer and others (forthcoming).
1/ Assumes corporate sector represents one-fourth of total GDP.

Caribbean. It should be emphasized that in addition to investment incentives, the gap reflects other exemptions as well as the efficiency of tax administration. However, it still indicates the broad scope of the losses.

Policymakers should, therefore, consider reducing the scope of tax incentives. Directing savings from reducing tax incentives to efforts to improve other determinants of investment, such as better infrastructure and institutions, could, on a net basis, improve the prospects for attracting investment. It may also be more effective to lower statutory tax rates, while broadening the tax base.

To the extent that incentives are viewed as necessary, there is scope for making them more cost effective. Reform efforts could focus on (1) consolidating incentives in the legal code to remove discretion in granting exemptions; (2) replacing tax holidays with accelerated depreciation allowances; (3) avoiding the extension of incentives to new indirect taxes; (4) introducing time limits on exemptions while grandfathering investors eligible for incentives being repealed; and (5) publishing the cost of incentives to improve transparency.

Regional coordination can help overcome the collective action problem associated with reducing or eliminating incentives. Harmonization, for example, through a regional code of conduct, should follow some basic principles: protecting the tax system in each country; maintaining moderate and predictable taxation; avoiding tax discrimination; and limiting tax competition while respecting national sovereignty. The success of such codes will depend on countries'

commitments as well as on the existence of effective enforcement mechanisms. The effort and time necessary to develop such codes should, however, not be underestimated. By refocusing countries' competitive efforts to attract investment more efficiently (such as by improving the overall business environment), regional coordination efforts can, more generally, confer significant benefits to both countries and foreign investors.

Trade Preference Erosion

Since 1993, the effective export prices for Caribbean bananas have been declining steadily, as the European Union has reduced preferential access. In 1993 the European Union removed internal trade barriers, exposing traditional Caribbean exporters to greater competition, although preferences were retained under the new common EU banana regime. In 1998, country-specific banana quotas were eliminated for all countries with preferential access to the European Union, which enabled more efficient African countries to gain an advantage over Caribbean producers. Finally, in 2006, the European Union replaced quotas for Latin American bananas with a MFN tariff of €176 per metric ton.

These trends are likely to continue over the medium term. In 2005, the European Union announced a four-year, 36 percent phased price

Caribbean Trade Preferences

Real Banana Prices, 1997 - 2007 (U.S. dollars per metric ton)

Real Sugar Prices, 1990 - 2007 (U.S. cents per lb.)

Sources: National authorities; and IMF staff estimates.

reduction for internal sugar prices. This implies a cut of a similar magnitude for import prices from countries, including those in the Caribbean, continuing to enjoy access to the EU sugar market at above-world-market prices.

While globally efficient, the erosion of preferential trading arrangements will lower the income of the countries that had been enjoying special access. IMF staff calculations suggest, for example, that the value of implicit assistance provided by the EU banana regime averaged about 8 percent of GDP annually for the Windward Islands of the Caribbean (except Grenada) and close to 3 percent of GDP for Belize and Suriname during 1977–2005. These estimates rely on several assumptions but indicate the broad magnitudes involved. Similarly, implicit assistance from the EU sugar regime has averaged nearly 10 percent of GDP annually for Guyana and 2–4½ percent of GDP for Belize.

For these reasons, the erosion of EU trade preferences has been, and will continue to be, very costly for some Caribbean countries, with significant adverse effects on the trade balance, output, and the overall fiscal balance. For St. Vincent and the Grenadines and St. Lucia, which depend heavily on bananas, output over the medium term could fall by 1½–2 percent relative to the baseline. Guyana faces a cumulative output decline of up to 6½ percent by 2010, as sugar trade preferences are phased out. Even in countries with smaller macroeconomic effects, the social costs can be severe, given the adverse impact on the incomes of poor rural households and aging farmers who have limited alternative employment opportunities.

Adaptation strategies will need to reflect varied individual country circumstances and could include the following:

- Targeted safety nets and other steps to assist affected populations. Transition measures are critical to help vulnerable agricultural workers cope with the decline in incomes associated with preference erosion. Such measures could include establishing narrowly targeted income transfer schemes within the overall fiscal constraints, allowing workers to continue participation in national pension schemes with lower or no self contributions, and providing job searching and retraining opportunities where feasible.

- Encouraging more efficient agricultural production. In some instances, remaining price competitive under the new trade regimes will likely require undertaking new investments, which can be challenging for countries with high debt and limited fiscal space. Asset sales and external investors can play useful roles.

- Shifting out of traditional agriculture, in other cases, may be the only feasible option. Continuing efforts to improve the investment climate, lower business costs, and enhance labor skills will help encourage a reallocation of resources away from sectors that are no longer economically viable. Indeed, St. Kitts and Nevis and Trinidad and Tobago have already largely closed their once-large sugar industries.

Conclusions

The current economic and political context provides a favorable opportunity to reinvigorate reforms and advance integration. Regional growth remains strong and the external environment is still favorable. At the same time, recent or expected political transitions and renewals in the region can provide the necessary popular mandates to implement deep reforms and shore up fiscal and debt-reduction strategies.

Financial Sector Overview, 2006

	Argentina	Bolivia	Brazil	Chile	Colombia	Ecuador	Mexico	Paraguay	Peru	Uruguay	Venezuela
Financial system											
Banking sector assets / GDP	39.6	39.6	63.4	56.7	64.1	35.5	24.3	32.0	27.1	67.0	29.3
Financial sector credit 1/											
Credit / GDP											
Total credit	26.6	36.5	31.5	68.6	48.0	22.6	45.4	23.3	32.8	24.2	15.1
of which: % in foreign currency	13.6	83.5	...	...	...	n.a.	4.3	30.9	48.3	59.1	6.7
Credit to the private sector	13.0	36.4	30.7	68.2	35.7	22.0	22.3	16.7	28.4	21.9	17.1
Credit to private enterprises	7.7	14.0	19.0	45.5	24.7	8.6	13.7	...	11.5	14.5	...
Credit to households	5.3	22.4	11.7	22.7	11.0	6.7	8.7	...	5.0	9.1	...
Credit to the public sector	13.6	0.1	0.8	0.4	8.8	0.6	23.1	6.6	4.4	1.7	-2.0
Credit growth (%), 2004-06 avg.											
Total	8.4	3.7	20.5	16.9	15.1	21.2	14.5	18.5	12.0	-4.7	88.0
Private sector	28.5	3.8	21.0	17.1	26.7	24.6	16.7	13.3	12.3	-3.0	78.9
Corporate	26.6	0.1	16.6	14.4	29.7	18.8	10.8	...	9.5	6.1	...
Household	31.6	6.4	29.9	23.3	22.1	35.1	30.3	...	20.9	-4.8	...
Public Sector	-2.3	-6.3	9.0	1.1	7.0	-20.6	12.5	37.8	10.8	-15.4	86.3
Mortgage lending											
Share of GDP	1.6	7.3	1.5	14.0	2.4	1.9	3.8	...	2.3	7.9	...
Growth (%), 2004-06 avg.	3.9	7.9	12.8	20.1	-6.5	39.5	16.2	...	15.8	1.5	...
Deposits											
Total deposits / GDP	26.1	38.0	25.1	54.7	23.4	25.1	16.6	23.6	19.8	51.3	34.3
Private deposits / GDP	18.7	37.8	24.7	...	17.3	21.7	15.7	20.1	18.4	49.5	34.1
% foreign-currency-denominated	12.4	76.8	0.2	...		n.a.	8.9	50.6	62.3	84.9	0.5
Interest rates (in percent)											
Policy rate, end 2006	8.0	6.8	13.3	5.3	7.5	...		...	4.5	...	9.3
Short-term deposit rate (local curr.)	6.5	3.7	12.6	5.4	6.8	5.3	3.5	10.9	3.6	2.3	10.0
Lending-deposit spread	...	...	...	...	...			...	...	...	...
Mortgage	3.4	...	...	...	...	4.9	9.2	...	...	...	3.7
Personal	19.5	5.3	39.5	21.9	12.8	5.6	28.1	10.7	34.8	34.4	
Corporate	8.7	...	13.6	5.0	5.2	4.0	...	5.4	5.6	24.6	7.4
Nonbank financial institutions											
Total credit / GDP	0.4	7.6	5.9	...	...	5.2	10.8	2.9	...	0.4	...
Credit to the private sector / GDP	0.4	7.6	5.4	...	...	5.0	3.1	2.8	...	0.3	...
Change (2004-06 avg.)	0.1	-0.5	0.3	...	...	0.5	0.3	0.1	...	-0.7	...
Mutual funds assets / GDP	2.9		39.2	12.1	...	...	7.5	...	...	...	...
Pension funds assets / GDP	13.6	20.1	16.1	60.7	14.1	...	7.9	...	15.4	13.4	...
Of which: Public sector assets	55.2	76.2	...	13.1	47.6	...	75.3	...	19.0	88.0	...
Corporate sector assets	14.4	9.8	...	27.4	19.8	...	17.0	...	43.8	3.9	...
Financial sector assets	20.6	11.3	...	27.2	17.9	...	1.5	...	28.0	8.1	...
Local capital markets											
Stock markets											
Market capitalization / GDP	24.1	...	66.5	119.6	41.4	...	41.5	...	42.8	8.6	42.1
Chg. in market cap. / GDP (2004-06 avg.)	-1.1	...	8.5	0.4	7.8	...	7.4	...	6.6	-0.4	9.7
Price growth (%, y-o-y)	49.9	...	32.9	34.4	17.3	...	48.6	...	168.3	...	...
P/E ratios	16.7	...	9.0	20.7	21.4	...	17.7	...	33.3	...	...
Volatility (30-day annualized)	18.7	...	17.7	10.7	18.8	...	13.0	...	18.4	...	...
Turnover ratio (%) 2/	6.8	...	46.5	18.6	27.8	...	27.6	...	15.0	1.5	3.1
Number of new domestic listings in 2006	4.0	...	30.0	7.0	4.0	...	4.0	...	3.0	0.0	3.0
Government bond markets											
Amount outstanding / GDP	28.4	...	48.0	10.2	32.2	...	18.6	...	5.0	...	9.5
Chg. in amt. outstanding / GDP (2004-06 avg.)	0.5	...	1.1	-5.9	1.2	...	1.2	...	0.3	...	14.6
Turnover ratio (%) 2/	33.5	...	0.6		115.5	...	...	...	10.6	...	...
Number of new listings in 2006	83.0	...	5.0	23.0	2.0	...	12.0	...	3.0	...	...
Growth in new listings (%, 2004-06 avg.)	231.4	...	-16.7	53.4	1.4	...	-9.8	...	-19.8	...	...
Corporate bond markets											
Amount outstanding / GDP	5.4	...	0.5	10.3	0.5	...	3.3	...	2.7	...	...
Chg. in amt. outstanding / GDP (2004-06 avg.)	-0.5	...	0.0	-0.9	0.1	...	0.0	...	-0.1	...	...
Turnover ratio (%) 2/	31.1	...	3.2		126.9	...		...	12.5	...	...
Number of new listings in 2006	529.0	...	71.0	447.0	24.0	...	88.0	...	79.0	...	...
Growth in new listings (%, 2004-06 avg.)	107.5	...	44.8	21.4	41.3	...	1.3	...	22.0	...	...

Sources: National authorities; World Federation of Exchanges; Bloomberg, L.P.; Bank of International Settlements (BIS); International Federation of Pension Funds Administrators (FIAP); Investment Company Institute (ICI); Shah and others (2007); Shah and others (forthcoming); WEO; and IMF staff estimates.

1/ Includes banks and nonbank financial institutions. Data reported for banks only for Colombia, Dominican Republic, Honduras, and Panama.

2/ The total share of value traded in 2006 divided by the average domestic market capitalization of 2005 and 2006 for Argentina, Brazil, Chile, Colombia, Mexico, and Peru.

Financial Sector Overview, 2006 *(concluded)*

	Costa Rica	El Salvador	Guatemala	Honduras	Nicaragua	Panama	Dom. Rep.	Jamaica	Trinidad & Tobago
Financial system									
Banking sector assets / GDP	62.1	63.1	60.0	54.7	58.2	133.6	34.8	62.8	50.3
Financial sector credit 1/									
Credit / GDP									
Total credit	43.2	49.2	39.5	51.1	33.7	97.4	19.4	42.9	36.5
of which: % in foreign currency	39.6	n.a.	37.5	30.7	83.7	n.a.	18.4	...	...
Credit to the private sector	37.8	42.9	31.2	47.9	33.3	91.7	16.8	35.0	35.3
Credit to private enterprises	15.7	...	0.0	...	17.5	42.8	12.3	9.1	22.5
Credit to households	15.8	...	...	...	14.7	49.7	4.5	7.6	12.8
Credit to the public sector	5.4	...	6.8	3.2	0.4	5.7	2.6	8.0	1.3
Credit growth (%), 2004-06 avg.									
Total	23.9	5.5	19.0	20.2	29.6	12.1	-31.4	9.7	11.9
Private sector	26.1	6.9	17.4	20.5	30.4	12.2	6.7	17.8	17.3
Corporate	25.2	...	...	...	27.7	10.3	-0.4	13.6	16.6
Household	24.5	...	...	...	33.8	13.6	46.4	28.3	18.7
Public Sector	19.0	...	30.1	16.1	0.0	13.2	11.9	-10.5	-18.7
Mortgage lending									
Share of GDP	8.7	...	...	...	4.5	...	0.8	...	3.6
Growth (%), 2004-06 avg.	29.6	...	...	...	41.5	...	109.6	...	17.7
Deposits									
Total deposits / GDP	46.7	38.4	41.1	55.6	41.7	143.1	29.2	41.3	36.8
Private deposits / GDP	43.6	32.3	40.3	52.6	...	129.2	24.5	38.7	32.2
% foreign-currency-denominated	49.2	n.a.	27.4	30.8	...	n.a.	28.8	...	...
Interest rates (in percent)									
Policy rate, end 2006	9.8	...	5.0	6.0	...	...	8.0	12.0	8.0
Short-term deposit rate (local curr.)	11.3	4.9	4.8	...	6.0	4.9	7.5	5.0	...
Lending-deposit spread	...	...	8.0	...	...	...	...	...	...
Mortgage	4.7	...	...	...	...	2.1	...	23.4	11.8
Personal	...	...	...	...	10.3	5.2	...	8.9	11.8
Corporate	9.5	2.8	...	...	...	2.9	5.9	8.7	...
Nonbank financial institutions									
Total credit / GDP	6.4	...	...	1.3	2.1	...	...	10.1	10.3
Credit to the private sector / GDP	6.4	...	...	0.7	2.1	...	...	8.1	9.6
Change (2004-06 avg.)	0.6	...	...	-0.6	0.4	...	...	0.6	-1.4
Mutual funds assets / GDP	4.8	...	...	...	...	2.9	...	...	...
Pension funds assets / GDP	5.0	18.0	...	19.2	...	0.4	2.1	...	...
Of which: Public sector assets	64.2	78.6	...	...	...	...	0.0	...	...
Corporate sector assets	2.1	0.3	...	...	...	...	1.9	...	...
Financial sector assets	22.0	15.6	...	...	...	...	98.1	...	...
Local capital markets									
Stock markets									
Market capitalization / GDP	...	...	...	...	...	39.8	...	55.0	...
Chg. in market cap. / GDP (2004-06 avg.)	...	...	...	...	...	5.3	...	20.1	...
Price growth (%, y-o-y)	...	...	...	...	...	...	...	11.1	...
P/E ratios	...	...	...	...	...	...	...	...	...
Volatility (30-day annualized)	...	...	...	...	...	...	...	14.2	...
Turnover ratio (%) 2/	...	...	...	...	...	2.4	...	...	...
Number of new domestic listings in 2006	...	...	...	...	...	4.0	...	...	...
Government bond markets									
Amount outstanding / GDP	23.2	...	...	12.0	...	...	...	71.8	...
Chg. in amt. outstanding / GDP (2004-06 avg.)	12.0	...	...	0.0	...	...	...	7.4	...
Turnover ratio (%) 2/	...	...	...	...	...	...	...	...	...
Number of new listings in 2006	...	...	...	0.0	...	...	...	45.0	...
Growth in new listings (%, 2004-06 avg.)	...	...	...	...	...	...	...	60.6	...
Corporate bond markets									
Amount outstanding / GDP	23.3	4.6	0.4	0.0	0.4	12.1	0.6	...	...
Chg. in amt. outstanding / GDP (2004-06 avg.)	1.3	0.6	0.0	0.0	-0.2	0.1	0.2	...	...
Turnover ratio (%) 2/	20.4	119.8	103.2	0.0	23.9	121.5	32.7	...	...
Number of new listings in 2006	43.0	10.0	2.0	2.0	1.0	22.0	0.0	...	...
Growth in new listings (%, 2004-06 avg.)	15.5	5.4	61.1	0.0	0.0	41.9	0.0	...	...

Sources: National authorities; World Federation of Exchanges; Bloomberg, L.P.; Bank of International Settlements (BIS); International Federation of Pension Funds Administrators (FIAP); Investment Company Institute (ICI); Shah and others (2007); Shah and others (forthcoming); WEO; and IMF staff estimates.

1/ Includes banks and nonbank financial institutions. Data reported for banks only for Colombia, Dominican Republic, Honduras, and Panama.

2/ The total share of value traded in 2006 divided by the average domestic market capitalization of 2005 and 2006 for Argentina, Brazil, Chile, Colombia, Mexico, and Peru.

References

Aiolfi, Marco, Luis Catão, and Allan Timmerman, 2006, "Common Factors in Latin America's Business Cycles," IMF Working Paper 06/49 (Washington: International Monetary Fund).

Alberola Ila, Enrique, and José Manuel Montero, 2006, "Debt Sustainability and Procyclical Fiscal Policies in Latin America," *Economía*, Vol. 7 (Fall), pp. 157–84.

Alesina, Alberto, Arnaud Devleeschauwer, William Easterly, and Sergio Kurlat, 2003, "Fractionalization," *Journal of Economic Growth*, Vol. 8, No. 2, pp. 155–94.

Alier, Max, forthcoming, "Measuring Budget Rigidities in Latin America," IMF Working Paper (Washington: International Monetary Fund).

Banco de la República, 2007, *Informe de la Junta Directiva al Congreso de la República*, July (Bogotá).

Baxter, Marianne, and Robert King, 1999, "Measuring Business Cycles: Approximate Band-Pass Filters for Economic Time Series," *Review of Economics and Statistics*, Vol. 81, No. 4, pp. 575–93.

Bayoumi, Tamim, and Andrew Swiston, 2007, "Foreign Entanglements: Estimating the Source and Size of Spillovers Across Industrial Countries," IMF Working Paper 07/182 (Washington: International Monetary Fund).

Becker, Törbjörn, and Paolo Mauro, 2006, "Output Drops and the Shocks that Matter," IMF Working Paper 06/172 (Washington: International Monetary Fund).

Berg, Andrew, Phillippe Karam, and Douglas Laxton, 2006, "Practical Model-Based Monetary Policy Analysis—A How-To Guide," IMF Working Paper 06/81 (Washington: International Monetary Fund).

Berg, Andrew, Jonathan Ostry, and Jeromin Zettelmeyer, forthcoming, "What Makes Growth Sustained?" IMF Working Paper (Washington: International Monetary Fund).

Braun, Matías, and Ricardo Hausmann, 2003, "Financial Development and Credit Crunches: Latin America and the World," *The Latin American Competitiveness Report 2001–02* (New York: Oxford University Press).

Canales-Kriljenko, Jorge, 2003, "Foreign Exchange Intervention in Developing and Transition Economies: Results of a Survey," IMF Working Paper 03/95 (Washington: International Monetary Fund).

Caprio, Gerard, and Daniela Klingebiel, 2002, "Episodes of Systemic and Borderline Financial Crises," World Bank Working Paper and database. Available via the Internet: www.worldbank.org.

Carstens, Agustín G., Daniel C. Hardy, and Ceyla Pazarbaşioğlu, 2004, "Avoiding Banking Crises in Latin America," *Finance and Development,* Vol. 41, No. 3, pp. 30–33.

Chalk, Nigel, 2002, "Structural Balances and All That: Which Indicators to Use in Assessing Fiscal Policy," IMF Working Paper 02/101 (Washington: International Monetary Fund).

Christiano, Lawrence J., and Terry J. Fitzgerald, 2003, "The Band Pass Filter," *International Economic Review,* Vol. 44, No. 2, pp. 435–65.

Clements, Benedict, Christopher Faircloth, and Marijn Verhoeven, 2007, "Public Expenditure in Latin America: Trends and Key Policy Issues," IMF Working Paper 07/21 (Washington: International Monetary Fund).

Corbae, Dean, and Sam Ouliaris, 2002, "Band Spectral Regression with Trending Data," *Econometrica*, Vol. 70, No. 3, pp. 1067–1109.

———, 2006, "Extracting Cycles from Nonstationary Data," *Econometric Theory and Practice: Frontiers of Analysis and Applied Research* (Cambridge and New York: Cambridge University Press), pp. 167–77.

Cubero, Rodrigo, and Ivanna Vladkova-Hollar, forthcoming, "Equity and Fiscal Policy: Income Distribution Effects of Taxation and Social Spending" (unpublished; Washington: International Monetary Fund).

de Ferranti, David, Guillermo Perry, William Foster, Daniel Lederman, and Alberto Valdés, 2005, *Beyond the City: The Rural Contribution to Development* (Washington: World Bank).

de Ferranti, David, Guillermo Perry, Indermit Gill, J. Luis Guasch, William Maloney, Carolina Sánchez-Páramo, and Norbert Schady, 2003, *Closing the Gap in Education and Technology* (Washington: World Bank).

de la Torre, Augusto, Juan Carlos Gozzi, and Sergio Schmukler, 2006, "Capital Market Development: Whither Latin America?" World Bank Policy Research Working Paper No. 4156 (Washington: World Bank).

Dehesa, Mario, Pablo Druck, and Alexander Plekhanov, 2007, "Relative Price Stability, Creditor Rights, and Financial Deepening," IMF Working Paper 07/139 (Washington: International Monetary Fund).

Disyatat, Piti, and Gabriele Galati, 2007, "The Effectiveness of Foreign Exchange Market: Intervention in Emerging Market Countries: Evidence from the Czech Koruna," *Journal of International Money and Finance*, Vol. 26, No. 3, pp. 383–402.

Djankov, Simeon, Caralee McLiesh, and Andrei Shleifer, 2006, "Private Credit in 129 Countries." Available via the Internet: www.doingbusiness.org/documents/private_credit_may07.pdf.

Echeverría, Rubén G., 2000, "Options for Rural Poverty Reduction in Latin America and the Caribbean," *CEPAL Review*, No. 70 (April), pp. 151–64.

Economic Commission for Latin America and the Caribbean, 2006, *Social Panorama of Latin America 2006* (Santiago, Chile: ECLAC).

Fajnzylber, Pablo, and J. Humberto López, 2007, "Close to Home: The Development Impact of Remittances in Latin America" (Washington: World Bank).

Freije, Samuel, Rosangela Bando, and Fernanda Arce, 2006, "Conditional Transfers, Labor Supply, and Poverty: Microsimulating Oportunidades," *Economía*, Vol. 7 (Fall), pp. 73–124.

Freund, Caroline, and Caglar Özden, forthcoming, "The Effect of China's Exports on Latin American Trade with the World," in *China's and India's Challenge to Latin America* (Washington: World Bank).

Gallup, John Luke, Jeffrey Sachs, and Andrew Mellinger, 1999, "Geography and Economic Development," CID Working Paper No. 1 (Cambridge, Massachusetts: Center for International Development).

Garcia, Pablo S., and Claudio Soto, 2006, "Large Hoardings of International Reserves: Are They Worth It?" in *External Financial Vulnerability and Preventive Policies* (Santiago, Chile: Central Bank of Chile).

Gertler, Paul, Sebastian Martinez, and Marta Rubio-Codina, 2007, "Investing Cash Transfers to Raise Long-Term Living Standards," World Bank Policy Research Working Paper No. 3994 (Washington: World Bank).

Gonçalves, Fernando M., forthcoming, "The Optimal Level of Foreign Reserves in Financially Dollarized Countries: The Case of Uruguay," IMF Working Paper (Washington: International Monetary Fund).

González Rozada, Martín, and Eduardo Levy Yeyati, 2006, "Global Factors and Emerging Market Spreads," IDB Research Department Working Paper No. 552 (Washington: Inter-American Development Bank).

Gourinchas, Pierre-Olivier, Rodrigo Valdés, and Oscar Landerretche, 2001, "Lending Booms: Latin America and the World," NBER Working Paper No. 8249 (Cambridge, Massachusetts: National Bureau of Economic Research).

Guerra de Luna, Alfonso H., and Jessica Serrano Bandala, 2007, "The Domestic Financial Position of the Household Sector in Mexico," in *Proceedings of the IFC Conference on Measuring the Financial Position of the Household Sector*, Basel, August 30–31, 2006, Volume 2.

Guimarães, Roberto, and Cem Karacadag, 2004, "The Empirics of Foreign Exchange Intervention in Emerging Market Countries: The Cases of Mexico and Turkey," IMF Working Paper 04/123 (Washington: International Monetary Fund).

Hagemann, Robert, 1999, "The Structural Budget Balance: The IMF's Methodology," IMF Working Paper 99/95 (Washington: International Monetary Fund).

Hamilton, James, 1994, *Time Series Analysis* (Princeton, New Jersey: Princeton University Press).

Hodrick, Robert J., and Edward C. Prescott, 1997, "Postwar U.S. Business Cycles: An Empirical Investigation," *Journal of Money, Credit and Banking*, Vol. 29 (February), pp. 1–16.

Huang, Yongfu, 2007, "What Determines Financial Development?" University of Bristol Department of Economics Discussion Paper No. 05/580 (Bristol, United Kingdom: University of Bristol).

International Monetary Fund, 2000, "Debt-and-Reserve-Related Indicators of External Vulnerability." Available via the Internet: http://www.imf.org/external/np/pdr/debtres/index.htm.

———, 2001, "Issues in Reserves Adequacy and Management." Available via the Internet: www.imf.org/external/np/pdr/resad/2001/reserve.htm.

———, 2007a, *Global Financial Stability Report*, October (Washington).

———, 2007b, *Regional Economic Outlook: Western Hemisphere*, April (Washington).

————, 2007c, *World Economic Outlook,* April (Washington).

————, 2007d, *World Economic Outlook,* October (Washington).

Izquierdo, Alejandro, Pablo Ottonello, and Ernesto Talvi, forthcoming, "If Latin America Were Chile: A Comment on Structural Fiscal Balances and Public Debt," IDB Working Paper (Washington: Inter-American Development Bank).

Izquierdo, Alejandro, Randall Romero, and Ernesto Talvi, forthcoming, "Business Cycles in Latin America: The Role of External Factors," IDB Working Paper (Washington: Inter-American Development Bank).

Jeanne, Olivier, 2007, "International Reserves in Emerging Market Countries: Too Much of a Good Thing?" *Brookings Papers on Economic Activity: 1,* pp. 1–55.

————, and Romain Rancière, 2006, "The Optimal Level of International Reserves in Emerging Market Countries: Formulas and Applications," IMF Working Paper 06/229 (Washington: International Monetary Fund).

JPMorgan, 2007, "Local Markets Guide—Global Edition," *Emerging Markets Research* (March).

Kamil, Herman, 2007, "Is Central Bank Intervention Effective Under Inflation Targeting Regimes? New Evidence for Colombia" (unpublished; Washington: International Monetary Fund).

Kaminsky, Graciela, and Carmen Reinhart, 1996, "The Twin Crises: The Causes of Banking and Balance-of-Payments Problems," International Financial Discussion Paper No. 544, Board of Governors of the Federal Reserve System.

Kaufmann, Daniel, Aart Kraay, and Massimo Mastruzzi, 2007, "Governance Matters VI: Governance Indicators for 1996–2006," World Bank Policy Research Working Paper No. 4280 (Washington: World Bank).

Kiff, John, and Paul Mills, 2007, "Money for Nothing and Checks for Free: Recent Developments in U.S. Subprime Mortgage Markets," IMF Working Paper 07/188 (Washington: International Monetary Fund).

La Porta, Rafael, Florencio Lopez-de-Silanes, Andrei Shleifer, and Robert Vishny, 1998, "Legal Determinants of External Finance," *Journal of Finance,* Vol. 52, No. 3, pp. 1131–50.

Lane, Philip R., and Gian Maria Milesi-Ferretti, 2006, "The External Wealth of Nations Mark II: Revised and Extended Estimates of Foreign Assets and Liabilities, 1990–2004," IMF Working Paper 06/69 (Washington: International Monetary Fund).

Lederman, Daniel, Marcelo Olarreaga, and Isidro Soloaga, 2007, "The Growth of China and India in World Trade: Opportunity or Threat for Latin America and the Caribbean." World Bank Policy Research Working Paper No. 4320 (Washington: World Bank).

Levine, Ross, 1996, "Stock Markets: A Spur to Economic Growth," *Finance and Development,* Vol. 33 (March), pp. 7–10.

Lindgren, Carl-Johan, Gillian García, and Matthew I. Saal, 1996, *Bank Soundness and Macroeconomic Policy* (Washington: International Monetary Fund).

Loayza, Norman, and Claudio Raddatz, 2006, "The Composition of Growth Matters for Poverty Alleviation," World Bank Policy Research Working Paper No. 4077 (Washington: World Bank).

López, Ramón, and Alberto Valdés, 2000, "Rural Poverty in Latin America: New Evidence of the Effects of Education, Demographics and Access to Land," *Economic Development and Cultural Change,* Vol. 49, No. 1, pp. 197–212.

Marcel, Mario C., Marcelo Tokman, Rodrigo Valdés, and Paula Benavides, 2001, "Balance Estructural del Gobierno Central Metodología y Estimaciones para Chile: 1987–2000," Estudios de Finanzas Publicos, September (Santiago, Chile: Budget Office, Ministry of Finance, Government of Chile).

Mulder, Christian, and Matthieu Bussière, 1999, "External Vulnerability in Emerging Market Economies: How High Liquidity Can Offset Weak Fundamentals and the Effects of Contagion," IMF Working Paper 09/88 (Washington: International Monetary Fund).

Österholm, Pär, and Jeromin Zettelmeyer, 2007, "The Effect of External Conditions on Growth in Latin America," IMF Working Paper 07/176 (Washington: International Monetary Fund).

Perry, Guillermo, Omar Arias, J. Humberto López, William Maloney, and Luis Servén, 2006, *Poverty Reduction and Growth: Virtuous and Vicious Circles* (Washington: World Bank).

Roache, Shaun, and Ewa Gradzka, forthcoming, "Do Remittances to Latin America Depend Upon the U.S. Business Cycle?" IMF Working Paper (Washington: International Monetary Fund).

Rodlauer, Markus, and others, forthcoming, "The Caribbean: Challenges of Integration" (unpublished; Washington: International Monetary Fund).

Sayan, Serdar, 2006, "Business Cycles and Workers' Remittances: How Do Migrant Workers Respond to Cyclical Movements of GDP at Home?" IMF Working Paper 06/52 (Washington: International Monetary Fund).

Shah, Hemant, Ana Carvajal, Geoffrey Bannister, Jorge Chan-Lau, and Ivan Guerra, forthcoming, "Equity and Private Debt Markets in Central America, Panama, and the Dominican Republic," IMF Working Paper (Washington: International Monetary Fund).

Shah, Hemant, Andreas Jobst, Laura Valderrama, and Ivan Guerra, 2007, "Public Debt Markets in Central America, Panama, and the Dominican Republic," IMF Working Paper 07/147 (Washington: International Monetary Fund).

Shin, Yongcheol, 1994, "A Residual-Based Test of the Null of Cointegrations Against the Alternative of No Cointegration," *Economic Theory*, Vol. 10, No. 1, pp. 91–115.

Solow, Robert, 1957, "Technical Change and the Aggregate Production Function," *Review of Economic Studies*, Vol. 39 (August), pp. 312–330.

Toro, Jorge, and Juan M. Julio, 2006, "The Effectiveness of Discretionary Intervention by the Banco de la República on the Foreign Exchange Market" (unpublished; Bogotá: Banco de la República).

Vegas, Emiliana, and Jenny Petrow, 2007, *Raising Student Learning in Latin America: The Challenge for the 21st Century* (Washington: World Bank).

Vladkova-Hollar, Ivanna, and Jeromin Zettelmeyer, 2007, "How Strong Is Latin America's Fiscal Position Really?" (unpublished; Washington: International Monetary Fund).

World Bank, 2001, *Poverty and Income Distribution in a High-Growth Economy: The Case of Chile 1987–98*, World Bank Country Report No. 22037-CH (Washington: World Bank).